Jesus Is Better Than Porn:

How I Confessed My

Addiction to My Wife and Found a New Life

G000080036

By Hugh Houston

Introduction

I understand. I've been there. The pull of porn enthralled me, then ensnared me and finally enslaved me. Jesus never abandoned me, but I was too blind, too afraid and too ashamed to seek out the help I needed. As you read this book, you will see that you and I are have much in common. I found freedom and a new life. I'll show you how you can too!

I understand. I'm not a psychiatrist nor a psychologist. But I know what it's like get to the point where you've lost hope of ever recovering your peace of mind. Perhaps you are drowning in lust, stuck on what feels like the eternal hamster wheel of compulsive addiction. Imagine how you will feel when you break free. Imagine a life lived with no regrets.

If after more than thirty years of being caught up in the lies of porn I discovered the truth that set me free, there is hope for you. In this short book I'll share with you the answers I found and the strategies I used to finally put pornography in the rearview mirror.

Pornography is reprehensible and unconscionable. To lust after another person degrades and devalues another human being as a "thing" to be used for our own personal self-gratification. Pornography is dehumanization at the most intimate level of our being. That's why it's so ugly. And in the end we dehumanize ourselves in the process. This is as far as we can get from the heart of God.

I chose to write using a pen name in order to share my most intimate thoughts while maintaining my privacy. This is not a book of statistics on porn. If you picked this book up, I imagine you are personally acquainted with this problem. You or someone you know is struggling, perhaps enslaved by the compulsive use of pornography.

This book is concise, practical, and impactful. I share my story so that you examine your own story. In these pages you will find hope —hope for a better tomorrow; hope for a new and better you!

There is HOPE for anyone enslaved by sin, because Jesus came to set the captives free.

- Learn how to fight lies with the truth.
- See how you can take control of your thoughts and your mind.
- Begin using your own personal "Battle Plan" today.
- Practice intentional living.
- God has already provided you with everything you need for your new life.
- Use the discussion questions at the end of each chapter with your group.

Freedom is a glorious gift from above! Let the jailbreak begin!

Table of Contents

Chapter One

A Deep Dark Hole

I felt trapped. I couldn't take it anymore, and I was scared to death. I knew that if I didn't do something quickly, my secret sin was going to get much, much worse.

I was 50 years old, and it felt like I had been fighting lust, masturbation and pornography my whole life. Up to this point our internet service had been dial-up. I had resisted getting a higher speed connection because I knew it would spell big trouble for me, but my wife and our son really wanted broadband. They kept insisting, so one day I finally gave in. Now with a high speed internet connection I feared my compulsion to search out pornography would get completely out of control.

For practically as long as I can remember lust had played a big role in my life. I recall playing "doctor" with kids on my street when I was about six years old. But my first real encounter with pornography came when I was a teenager and went to spend the night with my cousins.

My three cousins lived in another state, and I didn't see them very often. They were brothers who all shared a bedroom, and when I visited, they made room for me to crowd in with them. One night, we shut the bedroom door to go to sleep. That's when they showed me a tall stack of Playboy magazines in their desk drawer.

I had never seen one of those in my life. I still remember the rush of adrenaline that pulsed through my body as I flipped through several of the magazines, the images burning into my brain. Was it an addiction at first sight? I can't say. I know that in spite of the fact that I had been taught differently, from then on, I began to seek out opportunities to take another peek and feel that same rush.

I felt ashamed, but I kept wanting to see more. More than just my curiosity was aroused. It was a sensation I had never felt before. From then on, I began to seek out opportunities to take another peek and feel the same rush. (I had no idea that looking at those pictures triggered dopamine secretion in my brain which in turn produced the feel good rush.)

When I got my driver's license, I had a bit more freedom. Whenever I got the chance to stop at a convenience store, which in those days had men's magazines on the rack with everything else, I would look for another shot of excitement. I knew that as a follower of Jesus it was wrong for me to desire to have sex with these women, yet that didn't stop me. One day, when my sister had come along with me to a department store, she caught me looking at a Penthouse magazine. I was tremendously embarrassed, but not enough to seek help. The urge within me just kept pulling me back.

I was so conflicted. I had accepted Jesus as my Lord and had been baptized into Christ. I read my Bible. I prayed that I would live a life that pleased the Lord. I always treated women and girls with respect. Yet deep within me, my sexual urges were out of control. I was too embarrassed to talk with anyone about these feelings and as a result my feeling and emotions ran wild.

A few years later I went away to college, where I ended up studying theology and preparing to become a missionary. I fell in love with a wonderful Christian woman who is still my wife to this day. Like many so guys, I convinced myself that having a wife and a healthy sexual relationship with her would cure my desire to look at other women. I quickly discovered that I was dead wrong. I did not understand that just as it is impossible to put out a fire by throwing gasoline on it, desires do not go away the more you seek to satisfy them.

After we had children, it was not unusual for me to get out of bed late at night after everyone was asleep, sneak into the living room and flip through all the channels on the TV, hoping to catch a glimpse of something sensual or erotic. Now when I think about this I feel so ashamed and embarrassed. One year I went to a men's retreat and while there I felt so close to the Lord. I repented of my sins and renewed my vow to live only for Him, but when I arrived home late that night I turned on the television to seek out those lusty images one more time. What was wrong with me? How could I promise to change and then break my promise within a few hours?

Like so many others who are caught up in addictions of all kinds I believed that what was lacking on my part was sincerity or effort. So I believe that if I just prayed more fervently and tried harder next time I would overcome this compulsive sin. I did not realized how deeply ingrained these habits had become and that the solution would not be quick and easy. I also failed to understand that by keeping my sin a secret I was depriving myself of any help that I might receive from others who had answers for this kind of behavior.

When the Internet came along my problem got infinitely worse. Now, I didn't have to flip through channels to find something on TV or go out to a newsstand somewhere, hoping to find a magazine without a plastic cover on it. All of a sudden, what my sinful self craved was right at my fingertips, available with the click of a mouse. One day I was in my office looking at something obscene on a site and my oldest son walked into the room. I didn't know how to navigate out of it quickly, so I just reached up and turned off my computer monitor. Later I wondered what he thought, but not even that scare kept me from going back for more. The months and years trudged on with no relief in sight. How was it that my attempts to break free always failed, yet I never stopped to consider that I had to find a new strategy?

After binging episodes, before I turned off the computer, I would make sure to wipe my search history clean and erase all of the cookies from my browser. Then I would vow to myself and to God that this was the last time I would ever look at porn. This happened dozens, if not hundreds, of times. Each time I promised God and myself that I wanted out of this predicament, vowing that this time I would try harder and this time I really meant it. I now know that the worst lies are the lies we tell ourselves. It's been said that porn is a lot like throwing yourself off a cliff. You get a great rush all the way down, right until you smash onto the rocks below. Who in their right mind would throw themselves off a cliff for the thrill of the fall? But such are the highs and the lows of the porn addict. Porn promises excitement and ecstasy but in the end we are left exceedingly empty and utterly alone.

I was sick and tired of grip porn had on me. I longed for freedom. That's how the day we got high speed internet became a turning point in my life. I realized that if I didn't get help right then, my sin would get infinitely worse. I thank God for rescuing me and nudging me to finally seek help. On that day, with the Lord's help, I began to use the Internet, which had been a portal through which so much evil had entered my life, to search for ways to break free from this terrible addiction.

Why is porn so damaging? Why should every Christian and every human being fight to avoid taking part in this vile practice? In Matthew 5, Jesus discusses murder, adultery, divorce, etc. In each of these cases Jesus shows how these sins separate us from God because we are treating a human being, made in his image, as an object of anger, scorn, lust, etc.

Pornography is horribly hideous because it's impossible to live for God while transforming his children (our brothers and sisters) into mere objects. To lust after another person degrades and devalues another human being as a "thing" to be used for our own personal self-gratification. Pornography is dehumanization at the most intimate level of our being. That's why it's so ugly. And in the end we dehumanize ourselves in the process. This is as far as we can get from the heart of God.

How was it that after decades of determining I was going to quit and failing, this time I finally began taking concrete steps to breaking free from compulsive cycle of sin? What was different that day when things actually started to change?

Certainly, God was present. He touched my heart and planted in me a drive to finally search for help. Yet He is always there and certainly more than willing to rescue the perishing. I had become deathly afraid of my craving for porn getting exponentially worse. I could see I had to find help. I was desperate, like a guy who is drowning and knows he is about to go under for the last time.

I faced a dilemma, though. I wanted to confess my sin to a friend or to someone at church, but I was the pastor. . I was the one everyone looked up to, who taught everyone how to do what was good and right. How could I confess my hypocrisy? That fear kept me quiet. It wasn't simply that I wanted to avoid the public humiliation. I was concerned that confessing my personal struggles and sins people in my congregation would become discouraged or disillusioned. It felt selfish to unburden myself at the cost of harming others. I didn't know how to move forward. My dark, dirty secret was like an albatross around my neck.

Thankfully, I found a support board for men (and a few women) who were working to break free from pornography addiction. I read articles about how the addictive cycle works and testimonials of those who had changed their lives. I pored over personal threads and journals, where people wrote about their struggles and their victories. I began to go to the board every day and write in my own journal about my goals and my desire for a new life. It certainly wasn't easy to break free, but as I voiced my feelings, I began to find hope. I could see a light at the end of the tunnel.

Writing down my thoughts, feelings, and observations helped me see and identify my mistakes more clearly. My journal enabled me to discover where I had been going wrong and see what I needed to work on. I learned that by maintaining these sinful habits for so many years, I had gone against the values that I claimed to believe and cherish. I saw that I had swallowed many deceptions from the father of lies. One by one I had to identify those falsehoods and replace them with the truth and allow the Light to expel the darkness.

One day I wrote out a short list of lies I had often told myself:

- These pictures of ladies are harmless, really.
- Every man does it. It's just normal male behavior.
- It's okay to ogle women; I'm supposed to find beautiful women attractive.
- I'm not hurting anyone. I'm only looking.

- I'm not having an affair or involved with another woman. I would never do that.

If pornography and lusting after other women were perfectly innocent, why did I feel guilty and ashamed? Why did I hide these activities from my wife? Why would I go back and look time after time, when I had promised the Lord and myself that I would never go there again?

I resolved never to treat any woman as a sex object again. Instead, I would endeavor to look at all people; men and women, young and old, and see an eternal soul. Determined not to believe the lies any longer, I first confessed my sins and then abandoned them.

> He who conceals his sins doesn't prosper
> but whoever confesses and renounces them
> finds mercy.
> Proverbs 28:13

Author Edward Fudge wrote:

> "I have found that it is quite impossible for me to rise above sin in my own strength, and sometimes, like quicksand, it seems to gain power the more I struggle. Yet my experience is that when I yield to temptation, it is always because I DECIDE to do so. My will sins before my body does. I need supernatural assistance at the decision level. There is a way of escape, however, which is to put the problem before the Lord something like this, on a repeated basis, as often as needed."

> "Lord, I have this struggle against (X-sin). I cannot resist in my own power. No matter how I determine in advance when the moment comes, I find myself wanting to do the forbidden thing. I cannot desire to do the right thing myself. Lord, I honestly do DESIRE to do the right thing. I am WILLING to desire to do the right thing. But you must empower me to have a godly desire when temptation comes. I

yield my WILL to you. At this moment, Lord,
please work in me to WILL what you want."

Without a doubt, this is the very first step. You and I have to
long for a new life. We have to desire it enough to pay the price
and do whatever it takes to move forward into true and lasting
change. Are you willing to tell the Lord right now that you yearn
for a new life and are will do the work that has to be done? Pray
and turn your will over to the only One who can rescue you.

Renewing your desire for God's help is not a one-time event. It
has to be a continual process, one day at a time, one hour at a
time, one minute at a time. Today I pray that you will make this
decision to seek the light. I pray that you will ask the Lord for help
and take this first step down the road to freedom. Because
freedom is a glorious blessing from above!

Points to Ponder

Questions for Discussion Groups

1. Begin a list of why you want to remove lust from your life and break free from pornography. What factors have prevented you from changing in the past?

2. How badly do you desire to change? How will your life be different if you do? Make a list of all the benefits and blessings that will be yours as you walk in purity.

3. What makes sin wrong? How are our sins "crimes" against God and against other people? Confess your sins to the Father now.

4. Repeat aloud the prayer by Edward Fudge quoted above.

5. Memorize and recite Psalm 51.10
   Create in me a clean heart, O God.
   Renew a right spirit within me.

Chapter Two

You and I Are So Much Alike

Picture in your mind a hummingbird and a buzzard taking off from the same location and flying over the same landscape. They cover the same terrain, yet the buzzard only finds rotten, decomposing meat, while the hummingbird flits along sipping nectar from beautiful, fragrant flowers. Why would two creatures find such extreme opposites flying over the same countryside? Each one is looking for something different. Jesus said, "Seek and ye shall find." We all find what we are looking for.

When I frantically sought out help instead of hunting for things which would destroy me, I discovered there are plenty of resources available. In addition to the support board, I found a website called Recovery Nation founded by Jonathan Marsh. While Jon's experiences were not identical to mine, the situations he described and the feelings he shared were so similar, that I felt like he had been right inside my skin. He seemed to know exactly what I was thinking and how I felt.

I learned that the risk I experienced when trying not to get caught looking at the forbidden actually served to heighten the intensity of my emotions and make the forbidden all that much more thrilling and exciting. I had never realized this before.

One of the many lies I had told myself was that my need for sex was greater than the average person; therefore, if my wife did not meet all of my needs, then, of course, I was justified in finding other ways to fulfill this urgent "need" of mine. After all, God had given me this seemingly insatiable desire, right? What I didn't understand was that I was allowing these desires to enslave me.

I never stopped to consider how many people live just fine without sex. No one can live without water and we all have to eat to survive. Sex is a wonderful blessing from God intended to bring a husband and a wife closer together, but anyone can survive without it. We won't burst if we go too long without sex, nor will we shrivel up and die.

What helped me understand how this desire works was imagining a person who tries to quench their thirst with seawater. They can drink until they pop, but they will only get thirstier. Saltwater can never quench anyone's thirst; in the same way, the more a person looks at porn in an attempt to fulfill their need for intimacy, the needier they become. Worldly desires can never be satisfied, they always crave more and more and more. John D. Rockefeller started Standard Oil and was America's first billionaire. When a reporter asked him, "How much money is enough?" He responded, "Just a little bit more."

My desire to feel that rush again was certainly like this. I always wanted to see just one more image.

I had deceived myself into believing my desires were well above average, when in reality the more I thought about sex, the more I caused myself to think about sex. It was an endless battle, like pouring water into a bottomless pit or using gasoline in an effort to drown out a fire. That's why it's called an addiction.

Seeking help was my first step in breaking free from this trap. The second step was to break out of the compulsive cycle of lust. To break free from these old habits I needed to use "crisp boundaries" a term from a friend on the support board. In AA material they talk about how essential it is to avoid the first drink. Crisp, sharp, well-defined boundaries are essential to remaining out of trouble.

Writing to the church in Corinth the apostle Paul told the brothers to bring every thought into captivity to the obedience of Christ. Pushing every unwanted and impure thought out of our brains is essential to live a life worth living. The person who plays with fire will get burned. We cannot tolerate impure thoughts as something normal or unavoidable. That's where strict, crisp boundaries are a blessing. The sparks of temptation must be extinguished immediately before they grow into a raging, uncontrollable fire.

There were times when I reasoned that dealing with porn was worse than an addiction to alcohol or cocaine because everywhere I went, my thoughts went with me. I had a library of impure images filed away in my brain. How could I ever get rid of them? These obscene thoughts had invaded every corner of my mind. They were with me when I laid my head on my pillow at night and when I woke up in the morning. How could I avoid them? I felt like my brain was a haunted house inhabited by a million ghosts.

Here is the answer. Imagine an empty glass. It's not really empty, it's full of air. Now imagine trying to get all of the air out of the glass. You might try using a vacuum cleaner, but that probably won't work. The easiest way to get the air out of the drinking glass is to fill it with something else, like water. As the water goes in and the air goes right out.

That's what I had to do with my brain. How could I get rid of all of those obscene thoughts that hounded me day and night? I had to focus my mind on good things. For instance when a thought about a woman wearing a mini skirt or a low-cut blouse popped into my head, I would immediately begin to recite a Bible passage I had memorized or sing a song of praise to the Lord. Of course this took dedication and practice, but over time I developed new habits. I found I could quickly push lustful thoughts out of my mind by refocusing my thoughts on something wholesome and productive. As I learned to dwell on healthy thoughts, I discovered it was quite possible to win the battle against those lusty images that attempted to take control of my mind. The apostle Paul, inspired by the Holy Spirit gave this advice to the Philippians:

> Finally, brothers, whatever things are true, whatever things are honorable, whatever things are just, whatever things are pure, whatever things are lovely, whatever things are of good report: if there is any virtue and if there is anything worthy of praise, think about these things.
> Philippians 4:8

Motivational speaker, Zig Ziglar urged people to get rid of "stinking thinking". The best way to push all ungodly thoughts from our brains is to replace them with thoughts which are pure, true, noble, admirable, and excellent. Our primary battleground in the war against this plague (or any undesirable practice), lies in what we choose to dwell on, what we allow to occupy the space between our ears. We must drive out what displeases God and harms us by allowing God to fill our minds with only the best.

In 1427 Thomas A. Kempis wrote the following in <u>The Imitation of Christ</u>:

> "Above all, we must be especially alert against the beginnings of temptation, for the enemy is more easily conquered if he is refused admittance to the mind and is met beyond the threshold when he knocks. First, a mere thought comes to mind, then strong imagination, followed by pleasure, evil delight, and consent. Thus, because he is not resisted in the beginning, Satan gains full entry. And the longer a man delays in resisting, so much the weaker does he become each day, while the strength of the enemy grows against him."

This has certainly been true in my life. When I resist temptations right off the bat, I do just fine. But if I give in just a hair, leave the door ajar just a fraction of an inch, it soon becomes almost impossible not to yield. My best strategy (really the only strategy that works) is to avoid every impure thought and to stay as far away from the slippery slope as possible.

Filthy or impure thoughts cannot be toyed with. Only a fool tries to see how close he can get to the edge of the slippery slope before sliding down all the way to the bottom. The best way to head off feelings of lust is to nip them in the bud. Act quickly, vigorously, and decisively. Be radical.

Here is a great example of the kinds of changes we're talking about.

Autobiography in Five Chapters
by Portia Nelson

Chapter I

I walk down the street.

There is a deep hole in the sidewalk

I fall in.

I am lost...

I am hopeless.

It isn't my fault.

It takes forever to find a way out.

Chapter II

I walk down the same street.

There is a deep hole in the sidewalk.

I pretend I don't see it.

I fall in again.

I can't believe I'm in the same place.

But it isn't my fault.

It still takes a long time to get out.

Chapter III

I walk down the same street.

There is a deep hole in the sidewalk.

I see it is there.

I still fall in...it's a habit

My eyes are open; I know where I am;

It is my fault.

I get out immediately.

Chapter IV

I walk down the same street.

There is a deep hole in the sidewalk.

I walk around it.

Chapter V

I walk down another street.

The whole idea of crisp boundaries means jumping directly to chapter five in this poem. After all, you have probably been living in chapters one and two for longer than you would like to admit. It's time to wake up. It's time to look in the mirror and say, "The buck stops here! I am sabotaging myself; I walked straight into that hole. With God's help and the help of a few friends, I am going to make some drastic changes in my life. This has to stop!"

In my case crisp boundaries meant eliminating most TV shows these days, as well as most movies. My desire is to fill my mind with things that are edifying and beneficial. I discovered I had to avoid any kind of Google search for images, as well as YouTube. I always make sure to use Safe Search on these search engines. I always go to bed at the same time as my wife, to avoid late nights flipping through those TV channels.

If I aim at only avoiding the really bad stuff, but remain content to allow my mind to dwell on "normal" provocative thoughts, I will never find freedom. The beast of lust must be starved to death. I cannot continue to ogle women, look at promiscuous photos, or coddle impure images in my mind and hope to find freedom.

In my opinion, this is what has made this attempt at freedom different from all previous attempts. In the past, I would allow myself the "luxury" of looking when women were technically "clothed".

In reality, there are at least two things wrong with this kind of thinking:

1. I was still lusting by ogling women's bodies and degrading them as mere sex objects.

2. One thing leads to another, and I'd soon find myself at the bottom of a slippery slope.

This brings us back to the analogy of drinking salt water. One little sip won't kill you. But it sure will make you thirsty for more, and more, and more... For this reason, it is my goal to eliminate every sexually impure thought. As Paul wrote to the church in Ephesus:

> But among you there must **not be even a hint**
> of sexual immorality, or of any kind of impurity,
> or of greed, because these are improper for
> God's holy people.
> Ephesians 5:3

If I asked you to stop a mighty river from flowing, you would find it impossible. But follow that same river up to its source, where a little spring comes bubbling up out of the ground and try to stop it now—much easier.

In the book Song of Solomon, verse 2:15 it is written:

> Catch for us the foxes, the little foxes that ruin
> the vineyards, our vineyards that are in bloom.

The only way to develop clean and healthy thoughts is to ruthlessly eliminate every impure thought. This means changing the channel on the TV and turning off the computer or my smartphone whenever I'm feeling vulnerable to lust. It means looking away and not looking back a second time when a woman catches my eye.

By avoiding the "little foxes", things that most people would consider perfectly normal and okay, it is possible to avoid the slippery slope which leads to the slimy pit of sin. Of course, temptations will appear, but with God's help, it is possible to quickly switch my thoughts to other things - good and helpful things.

Thank God I've learned that change is possible, even for someone like me who kept making the same mistakes, over and over again, for close to 40 years.

We are all so much alike. This idea of crisp boundaries applies to every one of us. Do you want to stop worrying, quit being controlled by your anger, or eliminate lies from your speech? You have to go to the source. Where does it all begin? Work out boundaries that will keep you on a good path. Look at people with good eyes. Jesus said in Matthew 6:22-23:

> The eye is the lamp of the body. If your eyes are
> healthy, your whole body will be full of

light. But if your eyes are unhealthy, your whole
body will be full of darkness. If then the light
within you is darkness, how great is that
darkness!

The focus is: What am I going to allow into my mind? If I want
to walk in the light, I have to seek the light. I can never permit
myself to flirt with darkness, to see how close I can get to the fire
without getting burned. The wise person knows that a guardrail on
a highway is a good thing. Focusing my thoughts on good things by
listening to Christian music, memorizing Bible verses, or just
thinking about happy moments with my family is always a wise
decision.

The instant an unwanted or unhealthy thought appears in my
head, I force it out by choosing to think about something noble and
true. This was extremely difficult for me in those first days and
weeks. After years of allowing my mind to dwell on those pictures,
deep ruts had burrowed into my brain. By working diligently at
immediately controlling my thoughts, I slowly began to receive a
great blessing from the Lord: I got my mind back! Those impure
thoughts that had tortured me night and day slowly began to
recede into the background, and I found hope for a new life and a
new way of being.

Crisp boundaries mean setting up guidelines that I know will
protect me and help me. Perhaps I will modify these boundaries
someday, but for now, I know they are my lifeline. These
guardrails are my friends who protect me from the slippery slope of
doom. I ignore them at my own peril.

You may recall the story of Joseph and Potiphar's wife in Genesis
39. She would not leave Joseph alone, but he kept saying "no" and
refused her advances. One day when the two of them were alone
in the house, she grabbed Joseph. He didn't attempt to reason with
her; Joseph ran away as fast as he could. Precisely the advice that
Paul gave to the young evangelist, Timothy:

> Flee from youthful lusts; but pursue
> righteousness, faith, love, and peace with those
> who call on the Lord out of a pure heart.
> 2 Timothy 2:22

In regard to sin and seeking God, rigid rules and radical thinking are almost always our best course of action. In his book, The Purity Principle (pg. 53), Randy Alcorn puts it this way:

> "When it comes to sexual temptation, it pays to be a coward. He who hesitates (and rationalizes) is lost. He who runs, lives."

I learned a life-altering truth from the world-renowned psychiatrist Victor Frankl, author of the classic bestseller, *Man's Search for Meaning*. Frankl's personal story of finding a reason to live in the direst of circumstances, a Nazi concentration camp, has inspired millions. Dr. Frankl put it this way:

> "We who lived in concentration camps can remember the men who walked through the huts comforting others, giving away their last piece of bread. They may have been few in number, but they offer sufficient proof that everything can be taken from a man but one thing: the last of the human freedoms -- to choose one's attitude in any given set of circumstances, to choose one's own way."

In addition to the lie I told myself about my sexual needs being "greater than the average bear", I had also convinced myself that my desires were uncontrollable. I believed the lie that, in spite of my best efforts, this thing was bigger than me and I would never be able to overcome it. Dr. Frankl was the cavalry charging down the hill to rescue me. No, I'm not doomed to repeat yesterday's sins. God has given me the ability to decide and choose which thoughts and ideas I will allow to inhabit my mind. My ultimate freedom as a human being is to determine what I will permit to occupy my thoughts.

As Martin Luther wrote: "You cannot keep birds from flying over your head, but you can keep them from building a nest in your hair." Now I understand that if particular thoughts have made their home in my brain, it is because I allowed them to roost there. In fact, they may actually be there because I invited them in and made them feel right at home.

This strategy of quickly and ruthlessly throwing certain thoughts in the trash and instantly replacing them with beautiful, worthwhile ideas has served me well. Like a kid learning to ride a bike, I fell down many times. But I would just dust off my pants and get back on my bike and start pedaling again. At the time it seemed like an endless task, and sometimes, it felt like I would never make it. But I just kept plodding forward. With God's grace and mercy, I fought each battle in an attempt to win the war, and He helped me every step of the way.

These words from the book of wisdom helped me:

> My son, attend to my words. Turn your ear to my sayings.
>
> Let them not depart from your eyes. Keep them in the center of your heart.
>
> For they are life to those who find them, and health to their whole body.
>
> Keep your heart with all diligence, for out of it is the wellspring of life.
>
> Put away from yourself a perverse mouth. Put corrupt lips far from you.
>
> Let your eyes look straight ahead. Fix your gaze directly before you.
>
> Make the path of your feet level. Let all of your ways be established.
>
> Don't turn to the right hand nor to the left. Remove your foot from evil.
>
> Proverbs 4:20-27

The New Century Version translates Proverbs 4.23 like this: "Be careful what you think because your thoughts run your life."

You don't have to wait until you are 50 years old to get help. You can begin your new life today.

Points to Ponder
Questions for Discussion Groups

1. Read Philippians 4:8-9. How can you begin to change the kinds of thoughts you allow to occupy your brain today?

2. What are some things you need to avoid in order to improve your life and to avoid putting the wrong kinds of thoughts in your head?

3. Read Ephesians 5:3. Talk about how 99% pure doesn't exist. Why is it necessary to be radical in our pursuit of godliness?

4. Read Song of Solomon 2:15. What are some "little foxes" that you need to remove from your life?

5. Read Proverbs 4:23. How do you react to this verse? "Be careful what you think, because your thoughts run your life."

Chapter Three

How to Quit Smoking

Joseph Frascella, director of the division of clinical neuroscience at the National Institute on Drug Abuse (NIDA) wrote in Time Magazine:

> "Addictions are repetitive behaviors in the face of negative consequences, the desire to continue something you know is bad for you."
> The Science Of Addiction, Michael D. Lemonick.
> Time. New York:
> Jul 16, 2007. Vol. 170, Iss. 3; pg. 42

How foolish could I have been? Why would I continue to do something I knew was bad for me? I often rationalized by telling myself that it wasn't really that bad. I wasn't hurting anyone. I was simply looking at pictures. I would tell myself I was going to stop. I would vow this was the last time. This continued for weeks and months and years.

One thing is for sure. Until I really believed that this was BAD for me, I would never stop.

Allen Carr wrote the book The Easy Way to Stop Smoking. This book surprised me. The author is totally against tapering off and gradually smoking less and less. He tells the reader not to quit smoking until they reach the end of the book. Then he goes about showing how bad and silly smoking is. Carr explains how the whole idea of holding a cigarette in your hand expecting it to help you feel better or lessen your stress is ridiculous. Nicotine produces the very problems and symptoms it offers to cure!

What did porn have to offer me? Everything! Those images were so enticing. The women were so alluring, their smiles, so inviting. The rush which overwhelmed me was extremely intoxicating in the moment, but at what an incalculable cost to me and those closest to me! It is tragic that something which results in so much shame and regret is at the same time so irresistible. It was like being addicted to an electric fence.

The tremendous price I was paying for this momentary high is poignantly illustrated in the following story, The Skylark's Bargain by G. H. Charnley:

> "There once was a young skylark who was very fond of worms. He used to say he would give anything if he could only make sure of having all the worms he could eat. One day while he was flying high in the sky, he looked down and saw something unusual below. Feeling curious, the young skylark dropped lower and lower until at last he could see. And my! What a wonderful sight he beheld. There was a tiny coach, painted black with red blinds and yellow wheels, drawn by two magpies.

> Walking in front of the coach was a little old man, wearing a black coat with red trousers and yellow shoes. He carried a bell and, as he walked, he kept swinging the bell and shouting --

> 'Who will buy? Who will buy?
> I am selling in all weather.
> Fine and fat and juicy worms,
> In exchange for skylark's feathers.'

> The Skylark was attracted and flew down. 'Good morning, my pretty bird,' said the old man. 'What can I do for you?' 'Please sir, how much are they?' asked the skylark. 'Two for a feather and the coach is full of them!'

> 'Are they fresh?' 'Yes, indeed, they were all gathered fresh this morning'

> The Skylark gave a painful little tug at his wing and dropped a feather into the old man's hand. 'Two, please.' As the coach passed on, the skylark felt a little guilty, but he enjoyed the feast, and was pleased to discover that no one noticed the missing feather.

"The next day he flew with his father. 'My son,' said the old skylark, as they rose higher and higher, far above the tops of the tallest trees of the forest, 'My son, I think we skylarks should be the happiest of birds. We have such wonderful wings. See how they lift us up, nearer and nearer to God?'

'Yes,' said the young skylark, 'Yes...' But all the time he was watching a tiny speck which crept along like a black beetle on the cart track far below and he thought, 'I've missed the coach!'

So the next day he waited close to the road. When he heard the bell ringing, he plucked a feather. This one came out so easily, he plucked two more after it. Then he heard a hoarse voice shouting --

'Who will buy? Who will buy?
Surely we can come to terms.
In exchange for skylark feathers
I am selling luscious worms.'

'Three here' said the young skylark. 'Very good, very good indeed. That will be six worms. And here's an extra one for luck', said the old man with a chuckle. 'My word,' thought the skylark, 'that's a real bargain.'

So, the young Skylark became a regular customer. He found that he couldn't fly so high, but he didn't mind. There was less chance of the coach passing without being seen.

Time passed slowly by until one day when his wings were thin and worn and ragged, he suddenly realized he had made a terrible mistake. He tried to fly up into the warm sunshine he had once known but fell back to earth like a stone. Then he had an idea. 'Of course', he said to himself. 'Why didn't I think of it before? I know what I'll do. I'll dig for worms and trade for feathers.'

*So, day and night, he diligently searched and
gathered and stored. When he had amassed a
huge pile of worms, he hid himself in the tall
grass so the coach could not pass without being
seen.*

*When he heard it, he stepped in front of the
coach and said, 'Please sir, how many feathers
will you trade me for all these worms?'*

*But the old man laughed and drove off, calling
back over his shoulder, 'Worms for feathers is
my business."*

*So the young skylark died and was buried under
the green grass. And now they say that every
summer the older birds take the young birds
and fly mournfully over the grave, calling to one
another as they fly —*

*'Here lies a foolish skylark,
Hush your note each bird that sings,
Here lies a poor lost skylark,
Who for earthworms sold his wings.'"*

What a crazy fool I was! I was selling my wings for a pittance.
Yes, porn provided me with a quick fix, a moment of excitement
and an adrenalin rush. But rather than set me free, porn
imprisoned and enslaved me. Pornography is wrong—a sin against
God. This sin I chose to participate in takes human beings made in
God's image and treats them as mere objects to be used and
discarded by lustful passions. As I treated others as mere objects,
and at the same time robbed myself of the freedom which God had
offered me.

I was like a prisoner locked up in solitary confinement. I never
talked with anyone about what I was doing. As a result, I was left
alone to believe the lies I had come to accept as facts. Thus I
minimized, justified, compartmentalized and rationalized my totally
irrational behavior.

I justified my addiction with poor excuses. I didn't seek input
from anyone else, thus I managed to convince myself that pictures
of naked women weren't porn and that I was merely exercising the

natural urges God gave me. It wasn't until I finally worked up the courage to confess my sin to my wife and saw myself through her eyes, that I fully understood the emptiness of my rationalizations.

My wife helped me see everything much differently. She said I had betrayed her with hundreds, if not thousands of women. It felt to her as if I had invited these women into our home and had sexual relations with them. My involvement with pornography made her feel unloved, unworthy and rejected. I had never even stopped to consider such an idea, but when she poured out her heart to me, I knew that she was right.

I was once proud of the fact that I had never spent a dime to purchase porn, but in reality, I was afraid of getting caught. My wife observed that I was trying to present myself as the "good guy porn addict" when I was in reality just a tight-fisted porn addict.

I was like the smoker who finds comfort as he puffs on his cigarette. When my wife didn't seem to have as much time for poor little me as I thought she should, I could always find comfort from the ladies who looked so welcoming and affirming in those touched up photos. My head was filled with lie after lie. Here's the truth: sin will take you further than you want to go, cost you more than you want to pay, and keep you longer than you want to stay.

In a testimonial at the end of his book, "Pure Desire" author Ted Roberts described the lunacy of the person involved in pornography with these telling words: "I was involved in compulsive behavior. I was the producer, director, and star of my own self-absorbed, self-destructive disaster movie."

Allen Carr cuts straight to the point: I have to recognize the awfulness of my bad habit, how it hurts me and others around me. Otherwise, I'll never decide to go through the hard work of giving up my habit. I gave lip service to wanting to quit. I vowed to myself over and over again that this would be the last time. But I was not seeing straight. Too often I saw porn as my friend, my source of comfort, rather than as my enemy.

In spite of all of my rationalizations, this was definitely no way to live. I felt so much shame and guilt. I remember looking at pornography on a Friday or Saturday and then going to church on Sunday and taking the Lord's Supper. I fought to push those images out of my mind so I could think about Jesus and His sacrifice on the cross for me. I thought: "How could I have let this happen to me?" Even in my self-induced blindness, I knew I wanted out. I had to find a way out. Today I can say that I don't want to eat worms ever again. I want to be free. I want to fly!

A wise man is cautious and turns away from evil,
but a fool throws off restraint and is careless.
Proverbs 14:16

Points to Ponder

1. How do you feel when you stop and think about the skylark who sold his feathers for worms? How have you "sold" what you value the most for a pittance? What would your life look like if you were able to "fly"?

2. Do you agree with this statement: "Until I really believed that this was BAD for me, I would never stop."? Do you still consider porn to be your friend? What do you need to do to be able to see and believe that porn is bad for you and everyone around you?

3. Have you reached the point in your life where you are ready to say: "Enough is enough!"? Read Proverbs 14:16.

Chapter Four

That Guy in the Mirror

How did I allow my problem go on for so many years? I felt out of control. Like so many guys I've met, I remained entrapped in the addictive cycle because I convinced myself I was doing my best to get out, but when the urge hit, it was far too strong for me to resist. I had to face the truth about that guy in the mirror.

One day it was like a light bulb went off in my head. I was taking the free course on Recovery Nation, and discovered something Jon Marsh wrote. He said if I were in the middle of looking at porn on my computer and heard someone approaching the room, I would quickly close out that page and navigate to another site. I had no trouble taking control of a situation under those circumstances. Why then, when I was all alone and imagined nobody would find out, did I believe it was impossible to resist the urge to go take a peek?

The same thing is true regarding anger. I had trouble controlling my temper as a child. I thought that as I grew and matured I was getting better. But after I got married and had kids, I would explode at our children for their misbehavior or defiance. I could feel my blood starting to boil and my tongue would take over from there. When my wife confronted me regarding my behavior, I just made excuses. "Sure, I don't want to get mad and shout at our kids. It's not like I planned to lash out at them." She challenged me to plan ahead and think about how I should react in those kinds of situations and work out a strategy of how to handle things better next time.

Another example I think all of us can identify with is when two people are in the middle of a heated argument, and then company arrives. Most likely they will act as if everything is normal and nothing is wrong.

If I do actually have the capacity to control my actions in these situations, the truth is that I am always in charge. I am responsible for my actions. I wasn't forced to yell at the kids and nobody held a gun to my head and compelled me to search for pornography on the Internet. I decided to do it. Today I can choose not to do it.

As a person who believes in the God who created the world and made each one of us, I believe what the Bible says – "with Him all things are possible" (Matthew 19:26). I believe nothing is impossible for God (Luke 1:37). If I've been making all sorts of mistakes, who's to blame? It's that guy in the mirror! I have no one to blame but myself. If a bird made a nest on top of my head, at a minimum I allowed it to happen. I could have chased it away.

On Recovery Nation, I also learned about triggers. Perhaps we could call them hooks; those things that hook or grab your attention. You see something and it triggers the desire to go look for more.

I remember clicking on something I shouldn't and then in a flash, I was clicking a second and third time. It felt like it all happened so fast that I couldn't control it. I once referred to these as "mindless" moments. These were occasions where once I crossed the line, which could happen within just a matter of seconds, there was nothing to stop me until I had already gone too far. Somehow I just turned off my brain and refused to let reason have a voice.

For the person who is looking for an excuse, a trigger is all it takes to crash and burn. A trigger comes along and a binge soon follows. But none of this is written in stone. It is not inevitable. I had to learn that in actuality there are no "slips", only bad choices that I make of my own free will.

Jon Marsh says triggers are internal events, not external. They are perceived events and as such, the emotions associated with the stimulus can be changed. Jon found he could train himself so that the trigger would set in motion a new kind of response. Rather than allowing the trigger to set off behavior which goes against my beliefs and values, I can learn to see the trigger and use this event to move towards positive actions and healthy behavior. The process of rewiring or reprogramming my brain to behave in a different way is what recovery is all about. This is our challenge and our opportunity.

All of us do many things automatically. It's not easy for a child to learn to ride a bicycle, but with time and practice, the child can learn to ride a bike without even thinking about keeping his balance. It becomes second nature.

I remember when my father taught me how to drive a car. Our VW Bug had a stick shift. When I first started learning, I found it quite confusing and frustrating. To push in the clutch, put the car in gear, then step on the gas as I slowly let out the clutch, all the while trying not to run over anybody, was difficult. I remember how I tried to drive around the block in second gear in order to avoid having to shift to another gear. But now, it's a piece of cake! I can talk and drive, or listen to an audiobook and drive. It's all effortless. My hand knows where to go. My foot has been trained when to push in the clutch and exactly how to let it out at the right time, in just the right way. It's almost as if the car is on auto-pilot.

Another example is the person who is learning to play a new sport. The early stages of learning are complicated. What's the proper way to hold a baseball bat or tennis racket or golf club? Furthermore, if a person has already played this sport and learned the wrong way, they will have to unlearn what they had been doing wrong, in order to learn to do it the right way.

Bad habits are a curse; good habits are a blessing. In order to live the life I wanted to live, I needed to unlearn my bad ways of acting and begin to develop good habits. This required time and effort on my part, but the benefits made it all worthwhile. Just like learning to ride a bike, the person who wants to learn a new sport or acquire a new habit will fail. Slips and falls are to be expected. All that's needed is to get right back up and go back to doing what is good and true and healthy.

This is one area where I found my journal to be especially helpful. It was a place to go and write out what happened. When I made a mistake, I then had an excellent opportunity to analyze how it took place. What led up to acting out? What changes would I make to avoid "slipping up" next time? (Notice how we refer to it as a "slip", not as a "plunge" as if it were completely beyond our control to stop it.)

I learned to prepare for the unexpected; because the unexpected really can be expected. Triggers are everywhere. We live in a sex-saturated society. I had to prepare for temptations to pop up in unusual places, and always be ready to say a quick and decisive "NO!"

I realized that so many of my behaviors happened subconsciously, without me really thinking about them. Lusting had become second nature for me. I had developed the habit of looking for something to stimulate me. While I may have said I was opposed to this kind of behavior, my actions showed I found it pleasurable. In order to get rid of these bad habits, I needed to replace them with good habits. This is essential for anyone who desires a new and better life and can only come about through intentional living. New behaviors don't just happen automatically. I had to remain focused and maintain my mind in "battle mode" in order to make good choices quickly and easily. Recovery is basically the process of replacing old, unhealthy habits with positive habits so that the right thing becomes the "automatic" behavior.

All of this has been in the Bible for close to two thousand years. Writing to believers in the church in Rome the apostle Paul said: "Don't be conformed to this world, but be transformed by the renewing of your mind, so that you may prove what is the good, well-pleasing, and perfect will of God." Romans 12.2 In order to find a new life and break free from the old behavior patterns which had become my "go to" way of coping with life, I had to renew my mind.

As the saying goes, "failing to plan is planning to fail". While I could quote this saying, I was not putting it into practice in my own life. My excuse was that pornography just snuck up on me and overpowered me. Now I see I simply allowed bad habits I had acquired over time to rule my life. I had been "practicing" doing the wrong things for years. Now I discovered that the key to changing these habits is intentional behavior. If I just let things happen, I would certainly fall back into the rut of doing what I had always done. To begin a new life, I had to consciously relearn how to act. I had to think first and then act, not simply allow "auto-pilot" to take over. I needed to make a decision to do the right thing and then follow through with my predetermined strategy—to "plan my work, and work my plan".

When I talk with young couples who are dating, I like to show them two magnets. Hold the two magnets far apart and you won't have a problem. But if you keep bringing the two magnets closer and closer to each other there reaches a point where "zip" - they snap together. Hormones, feelings, and passions are even more powerful than magnets. They can only be controlled up to a certain point. If we don't plan ahead, act intentionally, and respect these limits, we are doomed to fail. We will fail every time. We can lament afterward that we didn't really want to do what we did, but because we made the decision to cross the line, down the slippery slope we went.

Most of the situations we face in life are not new. We have seen it all before. We need to go into the ball game knowing that the other team likes to blitz or that they have a really strong player. It is possible to prepare for triggers and be ready for them ahead of time.

The only way for change to take place in my life is for me to take responsibility. I have to recognize that I am not a victim. God gave each one of us the ability to choose. That means I'm in charge. It is up to me to learn from past mistakes, ask for help, make a plan and move forward to carry out that plan. And do all of this of course, with prayer and help from the Lord.

Points to Ponder
Questions for Discussion Groups

1. Are you to the point where you can admit there is nobody to blame for your sins but yourself?

2. Do you believe that God is ready to help you when you are ready to seek His help? Read Philippians 4.13.

3. Talk about one or two of your good habits. How has this habit been a blessing in your life?

4. How can keeping a journal and writing down what led to your failures help you as you strive to eliminate bad habits and acquire new, good habits? Why not begin your journal today?

Chapter Five

D-Day

Once I decided that I was fed up with pornography, I became obsessed with breaking free from my addiction. I searched high and low for books to read and websites where I might find help. One of these didn't have many members, but the pastor in charge of it was very proactive. Pastor Bill became my friend and encourager in my journey. He also kept insisting that I had to tell my wife about my involvement with pornography.

Everyone else agreed with him. Certainly, the wives and partners at the first board concurred. It is her right to know, they told me. How can you keep her in the dark? I even learned the term gaslighting, which has its origin in the movie "Gaslight" from 1944. In the movie, the husband tries to drive his wife insane by manipulating small elements of their environment and insisting that she is mistaken; remembering things incorrectly, when she points out these changes. To some extent, I was guilty of this crime because there was a side of me my wife could not see. Once she discovered these facts, many of my behaviors which had left her confused began to make sense.

One day I read this quote:

> "For a porn addict to change, he has to look in
> the eye of someone he has disappointed."

I had been working on my recovery for well over a year. I had made great strides, but something seemed to be holding me back. I needed to confess my infidelity to the person I love the most and to the person most affected.

As I look back on my confession, I'm not sure if I told her because she deserved to know or because I needed to get it off of my chest. I had put it off for 30 years. My pastor friend kept hounding me to tell her and I kept resisting. I told myself over and over again, "I'll just break free, and then since the problem no longer exists, there won't be anything to tell her about and I won't be hiding anything anymore." But my addiction kept rearing up its ugly head and one day I decided I just had to tell her.

Once I made this decision, I could hardly wait to tell her. I decided to confess on her day off. I found a time when just the two of us were in the house. That morning I woke up before dawn. I was so agitated that I couldn't go back to sleep. When she woke up, I took her into the living room and we sat next to each other on the couch. I then broke the news.

When she tells the story today, she says she was in a state of shock. It took several hours or perhaps even a few days for the truth of what I told her to fully sink in. Finding out about my compulsive addiction to pornography made her feel used, inferior, inadequate, and betrayed. I had always told her that she was the most important person in the world, but I had chosen the "porn girls" over her. It was almost more than she could believe and more than she could bear. She says it was like a dagger in the heart.

I felt relief; that I had finally done the right thing. My double life was over and the secret was out, but her suffering and pain were only beginning. She was on an emotional roller coaster. She has said several times how unfair this was—I was the one who made the mistake; I chose to do what I knew was wrong, yet she had to go see a therapist. She had to read up on this dark, perverted sin. She had to rethink our life together to see if any of it had been what she thought it was, or if everything we appeared to have together, was all one big sham.

We both became experts in an area where we would rather have remained ignorant. I discovered that in her mind my involvement with pornography was if I had had an affair or worse yet, multiple affairs. I had betrayed her and abandoned her to be with other women whom I found much more attractive and desirable. She was nothing to me. I loved them.

That's not at all how I felt. I wanted to break free from the pull of my addiction. I desired the real love and intimacy, which only she could give me, but how could she trust me again?

I learned that when a betrayal has occurred the only way the one who has cheated can rebuild trust is by being totally open and honest. I had hidden so much from her for so many years; now it was time for me to answer her questions. When? Where? How? What about this time and that time? She wanted to know what I had seen. She wanted to hear how it all began. She asked how I had hidden this for so long. She looked at me sternly and demanded: "Why did you never get help?"

There were a few times when she asked for details which I preferred to hold back. I told her I didn't think it would be good for her, in the long run, to have certain images etched in her mind because I felt they would be hard to forget. At times, she agreed with me. Other times she did not. I learned I had to respect her wishes. She was the one in charge of how to grieve this loss. She had the right to know about everything I had hidden from her for all those years.

This was a tremendous loss for her. Her storybook marriage had ended. She thought she was marrying a Christian man, a man with values. I was supposed to be someone who would never do these kinds of things. She even asked: "How could God let this happen to me? I went to a Bible college and married a man who said he would cherish me till death do us part."

Since this was such a gigantic loss, my wife was going through the stages of grief. The stage that appeared with the most intensity was the stage of anger. She was furious. Profoundly hurt. Horribly shocked. Words cannot even describe the blow that my betrayal inflicted on her soul.

The ladies on the online forum told me this would take time—years, even. And they were right. I knew I had provoked all of this hurt and pain. My wife's anger was normal and justified. How would she not be upset by my betrayal? I had not been the man she thought I was. I had sought out other women for pleasure and satisfaction. They had occupied my thoughts when I had vowed to cherish her and her alone.

There were days when she did not even want to look at me, much less allow me to come near her or touch her. I remember seeing her crying and thinking it was my role to comfort her in her pain, as I had done so many times in the past, but now, since I was the source of her pain, she did not want any comfort from me. A few times she was so angry, she told me she hated me. Some nights I slept on the couch. Her wounds were terribly deep. There were days it felt like the darkness had swallowed up all hope. I had to learn to be patient, to wait on the Lord, ask for His healing and allow her all the time she needed in order to heal.

One day my wife told me:

> "I trusted you, I believed in you.
> The man I thought I married would never have
> hurt me and betrayed me like you did. I am
> having trouble in my mind reconciling who I
> thought you were, with what you did time after
> time after time, all through our marriage. How
> could you let it go on for so long?"

One evening I found her crying and my wife said:

> "Every time you made a decision to look at
> pornography, you made a decision to hurt me.
> You chose them over me and were rejecting me.
> Every time you looked at porn it was like you
> were slapping me in the face or kicking me in
> the stomach.
> I trusted you too much. I was totally unprepared
> for this. I think that's why it cuts so deeply."

All I could do at that moment was to sigh and say I'm sorry. If only I had taken action sooner. If only I had not been so selfish, foolish, and afraid to tell someone or ask for help.

As my wife reflected on my involvement with pornography, she had trouble believing that I really loved her. She said, "How could you have loved me and done what you did?" I had no answer to that question. I was so horribly wrong, so utterly lost. All I could do was ask for forgiveness and a second chance; an opportunity to get on the right path and be the husband she wanted and needed.

For my wife, my obsession with porn was all very personal. I was choosing other women instead of her, looking at them and finding them to be sexy and beautiful. My choices hurt her. I was turning my back on her to look at other women. But I did not look at pornography because my wife is not beautiful enough or lacks sex appeal. When it comes to sensuality there is no one perfect person. When viewing pornography, the first picture of the first woman is never enough. There is an insatiable desire to look at another and then another. There is no such thing as perfection and no such thing as satisfaction. There is only an unending search for the next high, the next rush and the next thrill.

As I write this, Donald Trump is in the headlines because of at least two women he was involved with sexually after his marriage to his wife, Melania. Being married to a fashion model did not prevent him from thinking the grass was greener elsewhere. It's a sad, heartbreaking story. It's also a story that repeats itself in millions of homes across the globe every day. Betrayal is an epidemic which needs urgent attention.

Someone compared betrayal in a marriage to a story of two business partners. They've worked together for years, they're the best of friends, and they totally trust each other. Yet, behind his partner's back, the other partner has been stealing money from the company over many years. As a result of the loss of these funds, the company is suffering and may go bankrupt. When the guilty party finally confesses, how will his partner react? Shock and anger are inevitable; trust has been broken. One friend betrayed another. Restoring trust will take a tremendous amount of time and effort.

I learned that feelings come in waves. When it seemed like my wife was feeling better, all of a sudden, out of the blue, another wave of emotion would hit her and she would not even want to look at me. Those first weeks and months after I told her were extremely difficult for both of us. The Lord gave both of us the strength to keep moving forward. He gave me patience to understand, at least to some degree, what I had done to her, and helped her see that I really desired to change and become a better husband.

I saw the sun peeking through the clouds when a few months later my wife told me that I was now different from before, more attentive, more concerned, more present. I told her she seemed different too, more tuned in to me and more loving. She said that my being different made her become different. Then she told me she could foresee our relationship becoming better than it had ever been as we both strive to draw closer. In spite of the tremendous pain, she told me she was glad I told her the truth about my addiction. And she thanked me for all the work I had done fighting this sin and for the progress, I had made. Her words touched me deeply and blessed my heart!

Now that we are further removed from those sad, heavy days, my wife has said one thing that helped her survive was the obligation to get up every day to go to work and to help take care of our child who was still at home. Otherwise, she says, she might have just stayed in bed all day, or curled up and died. I am grieved that I inflicted those wounds on the person I love the most in this world.

Since telling my wife the truth, and seeing the consequences of my selfish actions, the stakes have become infinitely higher. I now see so much more clearly how destructive this sin is not only for me but for those I love. Now it's up to me to continue to make good choices one day at a time and to live according to my value system, with God's help! The Christmas after I revealed my sin to my wife, we decided to tell our oldest son about my addiction to pornography. He was home for Christmas and we took him aside so that I could confess my sin to him. His mother told him that she had agreed to give me a chance to put this behind me, but that if I did not, she would divorce me. That night he looked me in the eye and said: "Dad, you better not screw this up!"

Many people helped us along the way. A couple we had never met face to face mailed us a book about forgiveness. We learned that forgiveness doesn't mean you condone what the other person did, that what the offender did to you did not hurt, nor that it did not matter. Often forgiveness takes place bit by bit, day by day. I'll never forget the night, almost five months after I opened up about my sin, when my wife told me for the first time that she was working on forgiving me. Those were sweet words in my ears. I knew they were extremely difficult for her to say. I understood we still had a long way to go, but I was pleased and encouraged to see we were making progress.

When my wife made the decision to forgive me and to work on restoring our marriage I was extremely grateful. Today I am immensely thankful to have been given a second chance. I'm overjoyed to have someone believe in me and love me in spite of the hurtful, selfish things I have done. It is so much more than I deserve — it is a gift, a manifestation of grace. Thank you, Lord!

Points to Ponder

Questions for Discussion Groups

1. Talk about the benefits of confessing your sins to a person you trust.
   Read Proverbs 28:13.

2. Tell about a time when you were betrayed by a friend or family member. How did that feel? What was your reaction? Have you forgiven that person?

3. What does genuine repentance look like? How can you show a person you offended or betrayed that you really are sorry?

4. Why does healing require time? How can you wait patiently for the wounded party to heal?

5. Is there someone you need to forgive today? How can you begin this process?

Chapter Six

LOST

THINK BEFORE YOU LOOK . . . A LONELY LUST

The poem THINK BEFORE YOU LOOK, written by Daniel Henderson and published by Living Ink Books describes the struggle with addiction to a T.

> A man sits alone with a choice before his eyes,
> No one else is present as he wrestles with his
> lies.
> A fire smolders once again from deep within his
> soul.
> He can fuel its growing heat or choose to leave
> it cold.
>
> Passion begins to flow with a force against his
> will;
> Scenes that grip his mind bring the promise of a
> thrill.
> Emotions rage, needs unfold from a weak and
> lonely heart;
> In this very private moment, will he stop or let it
> start?
>
> A lovely wife, terrific kids have blessed his
> simple life;
> His gracious God and prayerful friends stand by
> him in the strife.
> But out of sight is out of mind in this moment
> of clear choice;
> Even the indwelling Spirit speaks with ever-
> fading voice.
>
> Images entice his spirit as their beauty pierce
> his reason;
> Setting aside real joy and peace, he indulges for
> just a season.

More brief and empty now seems the thrill once
it is done;
Regret and shame overwhelm as the lies again
have won.

He walks away so dirty, feeling lost in his
defeat;
Everything he really loves he chose again to
cheat.
Full of remorse in this return to the filth of
where he's been.
If only he knew how to stop this madness
before it starts again.

Being lost usually means I don't really know where I am. I struggled day after day, and year after year, going back to doing what I told myself I would never do again.

Since I had kept my sin a secret, I was all alone, without help. Stopping to ask for directions is good advice for anyone who is having trouble reaching their destination. Years ago, our family took a few days off to go on vacation. The place was about a four-hour drive from our house. My wife and I decided, spur of the moment, to cut our trip short. It was late in the afternoon as we packed our bags and got the kids in the car. Everyone was tired and ready to sleep in our own beds again. As I drove, I tried to go as fast as possible without going over the speed limit, but somehow at some point along the way, I had made a wrong turn. The faster I went, the further we got from home.

Many people live this way. They're going fast but they are headed in the wrong direction. Regarding my habitual sin of pornography, this was unquestionably my case. Telling myself to "just try harder next time" wasn't working. What kept me trapped in this endless cycle of despair?

In his book, Reliving the Passion (p. 25), Walter Wangerin, Jr. declared:

> "My denial of my sin protects, preserves, perpetuates, that sin. Ugliness in me, while I live in illusions, can only grow the uglier."

I was lost in my own denial and illusions.

Edward T. Welch, the author of Addictions: A Banquet in the Grave (p. 35), wrote:

> "Addiction is bondage to the rule of a substance, activity, or state of mind, which then becomes the center of life, defending itself from the truth so that even bad consequences don't bring repentance, and leading to further estrangement from God."

I was the definition of a hypocrite. I professed that I wanted to live for God and proclaimed that I believed in pure living and respecting women. I had never made a pass at another woman or kissed another woman, so I did not see myself as a hypocrite. In my confused, muddled thinking, I had compartmentalized my sin. I did not realize that pornography was like radiation, contaminating every corner of my life.

After I confessed my sin to my wife, I asked myself: "How could I have done something so unthinkable, to inflict such tremendous pain upon the love of my life, the person to whom I promised to be faithful and true?" But that's just it. I didn't think. In my own head, I pretended that this was my private problem and I was dealing with it the best I could. At the same time, I was trying to convince myself that it didn't touch the other parts of my life.

What kind of man was I? While I would never have admitted it, my actions showed that I was: uncaring, unfeeling, blind, stupid, ignorant, malicious, selfish, perverted, obsessed, afraid, proud, alone, self-deluded, lost . . .

Addicts are masters at compartmentalization. The dictionary says "compartmentalization is a subconscious psychological defense mechanism used to avoid cognitive dissonance or the mental discomfort and anxiety caused by a person having conflicting values, cognitions, emotions, beliefs, etc. within themselves."

In my mind, I was a good, godly man, a good father, and a caring, faithful husband—I just had this problem in one area of my life. I had erected a wall of lies around this behavior. This allowed me to lust after women in my mind and yet hold on to the belief that I was one of the "good guys" because I had not reached out to another woman on a physical level.

I was lost in denial. Treating a human being as an object for one's own sexual satisfaction is a monstrosity. When I convinced myself that looking at pictures didn't hurt anyone, I was only deceiving myself. How was I able to brainwash myself into believing that my fascination with pornography did not qualify as betrayal and adultery? Because this is what I wanted to believe. I had to close my eyes to the truth in order to live with myself.

My infatuation with porn caused me to close my eyes to the true nature of my actions and the consequences of my sins. By "putting my sin in a box" I deceived myself into thinking that what I did in private, behind closed doors, had no effect on my relationships with other people. Yes, I had a problem, but I was working on it and I was going to fix it.

In my self-imposed blindness, I thought my struggles with pornography were not really affecting my life as a whole.

My wife saw right through all of this. She did not have any problem seeing the truth. My entanglement with pornography permeated everything, and she saw how my whole life had been contaminated. In her mind, our entire 31-year marriage had been one big lie. I was a fake; I had been living a lie.

I realized it would devastate my wife if she found out. I knew it was wrong before God. I understood all of this, but only to the extent that I was too embarrassed and ashamed to confess my sin to anyone; I didn't take it seriously enough to actually do anything about it. I wasted so much time.

I was leading a double life. Sometimes I think I was not much different from a serial killer whose family and neighbors are all in shock when they finally learn what he did in secret.

Today I understand that addiction by definition is an irrational state. Psychology Today puts it this way:

> "Addiction is a condition in which a person engages in the use of a substance or in a behavior for which the rewarding effects provide a compelling incentive to repeatedly

pursue the behavior despite detrimental
consequences."

Along this line, Welch reasons (pg. 57):

"Perhaps no other narrative portrays the
irrational nature of sin more clearly than
Samson in Judges 13-16. With Delilah, his lust
defied all reason. Over and over she was
exposed as a betrayer, yet Samson was
intoxicated with her. Although aware of her
plotting, his desire still blinded him."

This certainly describes my situation when I was in the throes of
the addictive cycle of doom.

In Acts chapters 7-9, Saul had every intention of being a man of
God, even when he persecuted the early Christians; putting some
of them in jail and helping stone and kill Stephen. Despite his
desire to do what was right, in many aspects Saul was lost. His
good intentions and zealous efforts were totally off base. In his
efforts to do what he thought was the right thing, Saul was on the
wrong road, doing the unthinkable—persecuting Jesus himself (Acts
9:4).

I was more lost than Saul. He was trying to please God when he
persecuted those who believed in Jesus. I was caught up in
something I knew was wrong, yet I had somehow rationalized my
behavior and convinced myself that I was trying to stop. At other
times I minimized my destructive actions as not being really all that
bad. I vacillated between saying I had to quit and saying that
looking at other women wasn't really that wrong because I wasn't
actually with any other women. In reality, fantasizing about being
with other women in my mind made me an unfeeling and malicious
betrayer.

Part of me was walking around in the darkness, hanging back in
the shadows. I was always afraid of the light and what the light
would reveal. Now I see how the light I had feared was the light I
so desperately needed, in order to begin to understand where I
was, what I had been doing for so long, and find a way out of this
whole predicament. I was living in a fog. This fog cut off my vision
of everything—the bad and the good. I need the light that reveals

my sins because this same light shows me the path to peace and joy!

In my double life, it seemed as if there was the real me that loved my wife and my family and the church, but another me who was controlled by my desires. It took me far too long to discover how to manage these emotions and these feelings, in order to not be the victim, destined to do what I don't want to do, but I know I'm going to do because I've done it so many times before.

I read verses like Ephesians 4:18 "They are darkened in their understanding and separated from the life of God because of the ignorance that is in them." and Philippians 3:19 "Their destiny is destruction, their god is their stomach, and their glory is in their shame. Their mind is set on earthly things". Yet I never imagined these verses applied to me and my condition. I was totally off base on this subject, accepting a condition which was unacceptable. I lived in a perplexing state of darkness. My emotions and desires were out of control, taking charge of this area of my life. My habitual sin felt like it had a mind of its own. Without a doubt, the "god of pornography" sat on the throne of my heart.

My thinking was convoluted. Jesus said that "a good tree will produce good fruit and a bad tree bears bad fruit" (see Matthew 7:17). So what kind of a tree am I? Or better yet, what kind of a person am I?

A friend of mine sat down to examine how pornography had affected his life and discovered he had broken all 10 of the 10 commandments; the sins connected to porn addiction seem to cover them all!

Take a look at this list:

1. You shall not have any gods before me. – I set up pornography as a "god".
2. You shall not make for yourself idols. - Pornography was a big idol for me.
3. You shall not misuse the name of the Lord your God. - I denied God in my heart and thought that he did not care about my sin.

4. Remember the Sabbath day, to keep it holy. – Those impure images were in my head every day.
5. Honor your father and mother. – To my shame, I searched for porn in their house.
6. You shall not murder (or hate) - I've been hateful in my thoughts and actions.
7. You shall not commit adultery. - Pornography by its very nature means betrayal. Jesus said, "Whoever looks at a woman to lust for her has already committed adultery with her in his heart" (Matthew 5:28).
8. You shall not steal. – I looked at what was not mine and stole from others.
9. You shall not give false testimony. – I lied time after time to cover my tracks.
10. You shall not covet your neighbor's house or wife. – The definition of porn.

In my lost condition, I was not only betraying my wife, but I was also going against my own values and beliefs. How could I claim to love God and my wife, and yet be so callous to this problem? When I reflect on these things, I realize it is impossible to make sense out of nonsense. I had everything inside-out and backward.

I once knew a man with paranoid schizophrenia. He heard the voices of members of a gang with a plan to overthrow society. No matter who talked with him and tried to persuade him that these voices were not real people, that the threat was not real, he refused to listen to reason.

In a similar way, all of us must decide which voices we are going to heed, which voices are telling us the truth and which are filling our heads with lies. In my lost state of addiction, I had come to accept dozens of mistruths. I believed that I could never tell my secret to anyone. I was convinced there was no way out. I was trapped and doomed to keep repeating my errors.

I desperately needed to listen to the voice of truth. I longed for a compass to point me in the right direction and help me find my way home. I ached for someone to offer me hope that I could be a better person and live a new life.

This voice is the Good Shepherd who said: "The thief comes only to steal and kill and destroy; I have come that they may have life, and have it to the full" (John 10:10-11). Jesus also said: "I am the good shepherd. The good shepherd lays down his life for the sheep. My sheep listen to my voice; I know them, and they follow me. I give them eternal life, and they shall never perish; no one will snatch them out of my hand" (John 10:27-28).

Through his faith in Jesus, the apostle Paul wrote these words to believers like you and me in the city of Philippi:

> I thank my God every time I remember you. In all my prayers for all of you, I always pray with joy because of your partnership in the gospel from the first day until now, being confident of this, that he who began a good work in you will carry it on to completion until the day of Christ Jesus.

I'm so glad that the Lord does not view me through the lens of all my failures and my worst mistakes. His voice is the one that tells me my life can be different. He sees a new and improved me. His spirit is at work within me and will carry out His plan of redemption today and tomorrow. This is the voice I choose to hear and to follow.

Points to Ponder
Questions for Discussion Groups

1. Welch wrote: "Addiction is bondage to the rule of a substance, activity, or state of mind, which then becomes the center of life, defending itself from the truth so that even bad consequences don't bring repentance, and leading to further estrangement from God." Can you identify behaviors in your life where you still need to face the truth so that you can finally repent and draw closer to God?

2. Is it true that, in order for anyone to improve their life, the first step is to admit that they are wrong and need help? Where do you need to apply this principle in your own life?

3. Which voices have you been listening to? Which voices do you need to listen to? How are you going to put this into practice?

4. How does viewing Jesus as your shepherd impact your day to day life?

Chapter Seven

Me? An Abuser?

What happened with Adam and Eve in the Garden of Eden is often referred to as the "fall". But I heard someone say it would be better to call it the "jump" or the "leap". The serpent didn't have to talk very long or very hard to convince Eve that the forbidden fruit looked inviting. Eve didn't have a bit of trouble persuading Adam to do exactly what the Father had told them not to do. They did it of their own free will.

The words we choose to describe our actions reveal a tremendous amount about what is going on inside of our heads. All the guys on the support board would come and make a pledge to not look at porn. But it wouldn't be long until they would write in their journals: "Yesterday I slipped." Why do we pick that word "slip"? I know I used it all the time to describe my mistakes. I mean, it's not like I wanted to do it. I'm really a good person. It just happened! Oops!

Do you remember when Moses went up the mountain to receive the law from God, while down below the people were making an idol to worship? Moses arrived and asked his brother Aaron in Exodus 32:21, "What did these people do to you, that you led them into such great sin?" Then Aaron replied in verse 23: "They said to me, 'Make us gods who will go before us'". And Aaron came up with this story in verse 24: "I told them, 'Whoever has any gold jewelry, take it off.' Then they gave me the gold, and I threw it into the fire, and *out came this calf*."

I'll be honest with you here, this sounds just like me. "I just turned on the TV and there it was! I was surfing the internet and look at what happened to pop up!" Those are all such lame excuses.

I was caught up in an addictive cycle; I had created a pattern of behavior. My habitual sin had become an ingrained habit, but none of this can excuse my actions. I can try to minimize what I did by saying that I never went out with another woman; I can rationalize my behavior by saying that at least I was trying to break free from this habitual sin, that I really don't intend to go back to it. But none of this can justify the fact that I did not just slip. I jumped. I was a willing participant in this activity. I sinned because I wanted to.

I have read dozens, if not hundreds, of heavy, disturbing headlines in the newspapers. I can hardly bear to think about what one human being can do to another. Disgusting, horrible things. A coach or a doctor who takes advantage of young people who look up to and respect him. A priest or a pastor who uses his position to do the unthinkable.

In his book, "Sex and Money" Paul David Tripp describes a woman who has given her body to more than one hundred men in hopes that they might whisper in her ear "I love you." When I heard that story, I felt so awful. It's so tragic to imagine this woman reduced to such a condition. I was appalled as I envisioned a long line of men waiting their turn to take advantage of this child of God. How could they do that to her? How could they take advantage of her that way? But then it dawned on me that I was one of those men. I stood in line with hundreds of others, to look at those women who were exposing their intimacy to one and all. By my actions, I transformed a soul created and loved by our heavenly Father into an object of desire to be used and discarded.

Only the light can chase away the darkness. I need the truth, otherwise, I will remain enslaved by the lies of the evil one. I was blessed by the fact that the support board where I went for help had a section for the partners to write about their feelings. I reached out to those ladies for advice, and they were not afraid to give me the nitty-gritty truth about what I had been doing.

One wife wrote this to me:

> "Human beings are being abused to make porn.
> It's not okay for people to abuse other people,
> nor contribute to the demise of their souls,
> because I like it, or because I like to masturbate
> to it. We know ya'll like to call porn "it", and
> hide from the awareness that those women are
> not OBJECTS put here for your sexual

gratification. They are human beings USED for your sexual gratification BY you. In my opinion, the men who EXCLUDE their own contribution to this cycle of abuse, are far worse than the pornographers. Whatever is causing your blind spots is what needs to go because that is what blocks love."

Language is an interesting thing. We can use words to deceive and blind ourselves. I'm learning more and more about how I have done this. I used to say "I'm not hurting anyone. It is just me here with these pictures. I didn't talk with anyone or get involved with anyone or approach anyone. I would NEVER do that."

The truth is, what I had done in my mind and in my heart was far worse. It is absolutely essential for me to recognize the extent and degree of my actions. I was a participant in it and a promoter of this depraved thing called pornography.

I used to pride myself by saying that I had never cheated on my wife and that I had never so much as flirted with another woman. Well, this is what one of those ladies on the support board wrote back to me in this regard:

"If you've logged on and viewed pornography in your home, you have cheated at home, You have brought your porn girlfriends into your home. You did not go to a strip club, you brought a parade of strippers and prostitutes right in your home to perform for your viewing pleasure in private. Porning is way worse than flirting. You are having mental and emotional sex with those women just as if they are right in front of you. You cheated with hundreds or even thousands of women behind your wife's back. It sounds like you want to play it down so it won't sound so bad. You are just as bad as all the other guys who cheat on their wives in whatever form they do it. Adultery is adultery. Calling it pornography doesn't make it not adultery."

Today I confess that I used human beings as objects to satisfy my own selfish desires. I treated creatures made by God as something to be exploited and abused by me at my whim and fancy. And today, once again, I repent of this dreadful and obnoxious sin.

Open my eyes, Lord, to see where I was and what I did. Help me never to do it again. Help me to always treat every human being as an eternal soul loved by you. Forgive me and remake me! I thank you for giving me another chance to live a life worth living.

I made so many mistakes that I don't look down on anyone. You may have done things I never did, but that doesn't mean God doesn't love you or that there is no hope for you. Jesus loves each one of us and He offers new life to everyone. But perhaps you would benefit from more specialized help. You may have been viewing child porn, rape, bestiality, snuff, bondage or something else. You may have paid for sex, practiced exhibitionism or been involved in touching others in an inappropriate and unwanted manner. For these and similar cases you would be wise to seek out a counselor who specializes in Sexual Deviancy Counseling.

Asking for help is always the wise thing to do. And finding those who know what they are talking about and how to treat these specific problems is essential. If you were sexually abused at a young age you need to deal with these issues. Finding a professional who is trained to treat these and other issues will prove to be extremely beneficial.

Points to Ponder
Questions for Discussion Groups

1. Talk about Aaron's lame excuse in Exodus 32:24 "out came this calf". What lame excuse can you remember giving someone else or telling yourself?

2. Have you ever thought about sins or even crimes you might have committed, given the right (or wrong) circumstances? Say a silent prayer to God thanking him for helping you to avoid these grave mistakes. Ask him to help you keep your eyes open to avoid future mistakes.

3. Why is it so important to face up to the gravity of our mistakes and the consequences of our actions? What difference will this make in your life?

Chapter Eight

Working Your Plan

The familiar words of Jesus are 'Without me you can do nothing' (John 15:5). "But these must be balanced by the insight that, in general, if we do nothing it will certainly be without him" (Dallas Willard - The Divine Conspiracy: p.346). In my life, Jesus never let me down. I was the one letting Jesus down. Praying all day long to be free from pornography's grip on my soul was never going to help me until I decided to take action and take the steps necessary to seek a new life.

Is being transformed and finding a new life up to me, or is it up to God? My answer is a resounding "Yes!" The apostle Paul, inspired by the Holy Spirit wrote to believers in the city of Philippi:

> Therefore, my dear friends, as you have always obeyed—not only in my presence, but now much more in my absence—continue to work out your salvation with fear and trembling, for it is God who works in you to will and to act in order to fulfill his good purpose".
> Philippians 2:12-13

Verse 13 makes it clear that any progress I make in this life depends on the Father. He is the one who plants the desire in my heart, and I need his help in order to achieve anything good in this life. But verse 12 states obeying and growing are up to me. I have to work out my salvation with fear and trembling. I confess that God is too big to fit into my little brain. When it comes to theology, I can't comprehend everything. In my conception of things, this question has no either/or solution. The answer is both/and. I must work as if all growth in my life is totally up to me and my effort, while giving thanks to God because anything I managed to attain was only by his grace, with his help.

Willard uses the acronym "VIM", which stands for the words "Vision, Intention, Means" to describe the general pattern of any kind of personal growth or transformation.

Take the case of a boy who as a young person wants to grow up and become a medical doctor. The first step is to have a **vision**. I would like to help people. I see many people who are sick and I would enjoy being able to treat them and find a cure for their illnesses. The second step is the **intention**. One day I will be a medical doctor. Then comes the biggest step, because it requires the most time and work, of applying the **means** to achieving the goal. This young man will need to get good grades in high school. He will need to take all the math and science classes he can find. Then he will need to do the same thing in college as a pre-med major. He will have to give up some of the social events other college kids take part in, so he can study hard and maintain a high grade point average. Next, he will apply to a medical school and work for several more years in order to finally reach his goal.

Vision → Intention → Means

The VIM formula works with just about everything in life. Let's say a woman cannot bring herself to forgive her sister for a grave offense committed ten years ago. For ten years these two sisters have not spoken to each other. In order for change to take place, first, this lady needs a **vision**. Without the vision, nothing else will ever happen. She can think about how important her family is to her and how she needs to have a close relationship with her sister. She can remember what Jesus taught about loving everyone, even our enemies, and forgiving those who have offended us. Once she has the vision of how great it would be to renew her friendship with her sister, she needs to make the **decision** to act. If it is still too hard to forgive her sister, she can begin by praying for God to bless her sister, that God will work in her own heart to see the good in her sister, praying to understand the truth that everyone makes mistakes and we all need to be forgiven. As she works out the **means** on a day to day basis, she will eventually come to the place where she can look at her sister in the eye and say: "I forgive you! Please forgive me for being so slow to open my heart and reach out to you."

Over the past fifteen years I've seen scores of guys go to sites that help people who long to break free from addiction to pornography. I've also talked with several men face to face. I notice the great distress they feel. They are consumed by their lusts and desires, overwhelmed with the guilt and shame that follows. If there is a bright side to this story it is that, in spite of the fact that society and the media bombard us with the idea that the human body is beautiful and should be admired and that sex between two consenting adults is healthy and normal, these men still know first-hand something has gone haywire.

These men look in the mirror and realize that their lusts and passions have gotten totally out of control. Some have actually hurt themselves physically because their addiction to masturbation is unstoppable. How can something which is touted to be so fantastic in Playboy magazine or even in the Sports Illustrated swimsuit edition, make an absolute wreck out of so many lives?

Some men know that using a woman as a sex object is wrong because they read it in the Bible, but others who have never looked at God's word have discovered from personal experience the damaging effects this cycle of lust has caused in their own lives and in their relationships with the women they love. To me, the positive part of this story is that thousands of men from all walks of life, from teenagers to retired men, are crying out: "Please help me stop!"

What breaks my heart is that, as the weeks and months go by, I see these guys come and proclaim their eagerness to begin anew. They come and post: "One day clean!" "Two days with no porn." "One week with no porn and no masturbation". There are threads where everyone commits to 30 days clean or 100 days clean. And everyone rejoices when a fellow struggler actually reaches one of these milestones. But more common is the guy who remained clean for a week or two, or maybe even three, and then says: "I slipped. Back to square one." It's so terribly tragic!

You and I must look deeply into our souls to see if we really desire to change. As Willard wrote in an article entitled: Beyond Pornography: Spiritual Formation Studied in a Particular Case:

> "Most people involved with the use of
> pornography have not come to the place where

they desire not to desire it. For whatever reasons, they think it is too important to them and that they would be "missing out" if they did not have the desire for it. That concession traps them into continued use. It is like people who cannot imagine what it would be like not to be angry. It is so much a part of their life that they would not know who they were without it. Their identity is tied up with their desires. So, a person involved with pornography may wish they did not do what they do, but they have to go deeper. They have to be willing not to have the desires that they now have." (Journal of Spiritual Formation & Soul Care 2016, Vol. 9, No. 1,5-17).

That's why I've spent so much time in this book describing how vile and terrible pornography is and the countless ways it harms and destroys everyone involved. It is imperative that you and I view pornography as it really is. We must recognize all the pain and damage it inflicts. Only then will this activity which formerly fascinated our imagination become something practically unimaginable to participate in.

Obviously, any new project, be it learning to play tennis or ride a bike, will always include failure. However, it is essential to realize that a "slip" didn't just happen—it is part of a sequence of events. If I don't stop and analyze what happened and how it happened, and perhaps even get feedback from a wise friend on why it happened, then I'm doomed to keep repeating the same mistakes over and over again. Just getting up and determining to try harder next time will not be enough—it will never work. Trust me. I know from experience, and I'm guessing you do, too!

That's why it's necessary to take the time to think about and write out what some would term a "battle plan". You need "to plan your work and work your plan". If you really have a vision and want a new life, if you are sick and tired of being in a dark hole and you desire with all of your heart to walk in the light, then it's time to be intentional and think about how you are going to get there. What steps do you need to take today, tomorrow and the next day in order to reach your goal?

To simply proclaim "Now, I'm going to stop this for the next thirty days", without any kind of a plan as to how to reach this goal is like trying to build a house on the sand. A house without a solid foundation will never withstand the winds and storms which are bound to appear. There has to be a "how". Intentional living entails working out the **means**, day in and day out. Jesus said: "Seek and you will find. Knock and the door will be opened to you." Well, the reverse is also true. Don't seek and you will never find. Don't knock and you will remain out in the cold all night long.

I love sports. Years ago, a man I respected told me the sports section of the newspaper is the best place to find some good news. Most headlines tout tragedies and problems. But the sports section will often relate a story with a happy ending. Take the athlete who has a dream of someday winning a gold medal. He decides to go for it. Now, what will this entail over the next year or the next five years? What kind of diet? What kind of training? In order to attain his goal of going to the Olympics and bringing home a gold medal, this athlete will endure blood, sweat, and tears. And if he reaches his goal, you will hear him declare in the interview: "It was all worth it. Every sacrifice I made, all the hard work I put in, helped me win this medal!"

In Sports Illustrated, Trevor Moawad, a consultant in sports physiology, described a conversation with former Olympic sprinter Michael Johnson:

> "Early on, he identified what it took to be No. 1 in the world," Moawad says. "We talk about the illusion of choice. You don't really have a wide set of choices if you want to make it to the top. Michael Johnson used to always say distractions are the enemy of an elite athlete. Discipline is the willingness not to do certain things. If I have a bag of Doritos in my left hand and an apple in my right hand, you probably wouldn't need a nutritionist to tell you which was better for you. So why would you choose the apple? Most of sports comes down to simple choices like that. I think we want to make it seem complicated, but the reality is, it's doing the simple things savagely well. If I form

a habit, that habit forms me, good or bad.
Without sticking to the plan, there is little point
in having one."

If I want to live a life worth living, I must develop good, healthy habits and practice living out those habits, one at a time, day in and day out. It is essential to keep rehearsing the right thing, the right way, time after time, after time. Then, slowly, the bad habits which kept me trapped in the old ruts will fly right out the window and my new, good habits will keep me on track, even when the going gets rough. This is now the new normal! It's what I always do! Now it feels natural. It's my new autopilot. My new habits move me toward my goal of pleasing God and living right.

Your battle plan might look something like this:

1. Get rid of everything you might have related to porn—pictures, movies, links, etc.
2. Write in a journal every day about your feelings, goals, struggles, and successes.
3. Talk with someone who can help to hold you accountable and encourage you.
4. Read good books, take online courses, join a support group, etc.
5. Remember, it's not enough to stop doing what's wrong. In order to become a better person, it is imperative that you fill your soul with that which only the Lord can give. Read and meditate on God's word.
6. Memorize key Bible verses.
7. Talk with the Lord in prayer.
8. Work on improving your relationship with your spouse. Have fun together. Serve others together. Show your love in the little things—small acts of kindness.
9. Exercise. Get out into nature, volunteer for a project, look for ways to help others.
10. Dig deeper in order to understand yourself and what led you to feel the need for this addiction. Counseling is a good idea.
11. Plan out how you will deal with temptations and triggers before they happen.

Ask yourself questions like these:

1. **ENVIRONMENT**: What do I have within my environment that might cause me to struggle? What can I do to protect my recovery? What changes do I need to make?

2. **SITUATIONS**: What kind of situations do I find most tempting? What is consistent about these situations? What makes them problematic? How do I need to deal with situations like these the next time they arise?

3. **EMOTIONS**: What emotional states leave me the most vulnerable? Is it when I am lonely, stressed, tired, angry, bored, etc.? What healthy alternatives do I have for dealing with these emotions? Who can I talk with when I need help?

4. **BEHAVIOR**: What behaviors do I recognize as preceding moments where I am tempted? What actions can I take when I see this process beginning?

5. **THOUGHTS**: What patterns of thought do I recognize as leading me to moments of weakness? How can I act decisively to change or remove these thoughts from my mind?

6. **PEOPLE**: Are there people in my life who encourage me to do what I don't want to do? How can I address this? Can I avoid them altogether? Who do I know who can help me? What can I do to spend more time with the people who can help me?

7. **SUPPORT**: What structures of support do I have in place for my new life? How can I make them better or stronger? What new structures of support can I add that will lend strength to the existing ones?

8. **DEEPER**: Why do I have this problem? Why did I seek it? What needs does it promise to fill? What really happens when I look? What are the consequences? How does it happen? Why do I want to change? How can I change?

I heard that a winner is a loser who keeps trying. Like everything worthwhile, building a life worth living requires time, effort, and perseverance. Permanent changes will not take place overnight. Have you heard how to eat an elephant? One bite at a time! Recovery is that way. It's necessary to take small steps day by day, always with an eye on the finish line. Understand that changing lifelong habits is more like running a marathon than a sprint. This process with take many months, perhaps a few years. But breaking free from habitual sin and finding a new life is more than worth all the effort required.

Seeing a counselor or therapist can also be very productive. If you can find a person who has expertise in addiction, they will be intimately familiar with addict talk, and call the addict on it, rather than potentially be fooled by it. The therapist will know how to help the addict heal by getting at the root of the addiction. I believe most addicts are addicts because they don't know how to cope with life very well. The addiction provides a temporary escape from life's problems. A trained therapist can help the addict develop strategies to successfully cope with life and their relationships with other people.

Twelve-step groups provide a systematic path to ending addictive behaviors. Many people find a twelve-step meeting to be a comfortable and safe place to be totally honest with themselves and with others. It's not a place to judge others. On a basic level, everyone understands everyone else, regardless of the specific nature of their addictive behavior. When a person has not yet learned to be honest with themselves and comes to the meeting telling half-truths or blaming others for their circumstances, generally someone will call them on it, in a compassionate way.

These meetings provide an opportunity to receive support as well as to give support to others. Since being an addict is an act of selfishness, having the opportunity to help and support others is quite beneficial. Usually, a new member of the group will find a sponsor, which is someone who is more experienced and can help them walk through the steps to recovery. There are various twelve-step sex addiction groups, such as Sexaholics Anonymous (SA), Sex Addicts Anonymous (SAA), Sex and Love Addicts Anonymous (SLAA).

Celebrate Recovery is a Christ-centered twelve-step recovery program aimed at all "hurts, habits, and hang-ups", including high anxiety; co-dependency; compulsive behaviors; sex addiction; gambling; drug and alcohol addictions; and eating disorders.

From my background of having dealt with a secret sin for decades, I have come to see the importance of talking about my weaknesses, admitting my mistakes, and asking for help. The counselor I saw for a few months told me that Freud said "talking cures". Talking helps lessen my anxiety as I open up about my feelings. For me, it was important to voice my mistakes and get them out in the open. Saying it all out loud to another person forced me to face the severity of what I had done and my drastic need to make real and lasting changes. For me to look my therapist in the eye and confess that I looked at pictures of naked women and then fantasized about being with them while I masturbated to reach orgasm was extremely difficult. Yet what better way to eliminate all of my minimizing and rationalizing?

Of course, all of us who are disciples of Jesus know that he has placed us in a family called the church. There we have brothers and sisters who like us, are striving to live for Jesus, but like us, they have their own weaknesses, challenges, and struggles. I pray that the church can be a place for you and me to confess our sins one to another, pray with each other and find healing. This is certainly part of what the Lord had in mind when he placed us in this spiritual community.

> Confess your trespasses to one another, and pray for one another, that you may be healed. The effective, fervent prayer of a righteous man avails much.
> James 5:16

I compare talking with a sponsor or a therapist or a good friend to looking in a mirror. I may have a dirty spot on my face, but without the mirror, or another person to point it out to me, I am unaware of this fact. If I ever want to grow and improve as a person, I need people in my life who can help me look at myself in the mirror and perceive my actions as they really are. It doesn't do me any good to be surrounded by people who tell me what a great guy I am when my life is in shambles. It is essential to talk with people who will point me to the truth and help me face reality. Willard said reality is what you run into when you are wrong. A friend told me: "The truth hurts, but lies kill."

Points to Ponder
Questions for Discussion Groups

1. How can you apply "vision, intention, and means" to the changes you want to make in your life?

2. If you really do have the vision and intention, then sit down and write out your "battle plan" of how you are going to see this through. What practical steps will you take day by day in order to reach your goal? Make this as simple, direct, and practical as possible. Think of the steps an athlete will take in order to win a gold medal.

3. How can sharing your goals with a friend or a support group help keep you honest and motivated to persevere? If you still haven't found someone to help you on your journey, don't you think it's about time?

Chapter Nine

The Hook

Today as I look back on the years I spent caught up in the addictive cycle, it is easier to see how it all started. This knowledge helps me understand the traps which must be avoided.

One day I was walking down a street in a major city where only pedestrians were allowed. The street was lined with peddlers hawking their wares. I was taking quick steps thinking about reaching my destination. One vendor was selling wands which make dozens of bubbles with one swinging motion. He was demonstrating how they work. Right before I got to where he was located, he swung his arm and produced a flock of bubbles that glistened in the sunlight. A big, shiny bubble floated right in front of my face. Instinctively I reached out and grabbed the bubble with my hand. Of course, the bubble burst and when I opened my hand it was empty.

I have often thought of that bubble as a metaphor for the illusion of sin. Sin looks so attractive and appealing. It promises to satisfy all my desires. But these are empty, hollow promises.

The book of Proverbs portrays this principle vividly:

> Do not gaze at wine when it is red, when it sparkles in the cup, when it goes down smoothly!
>
> In the end it bites like a snake and poisons like a viper.
>
> Your eyes will see strange sights, and your mind will imagine confusing things.
>
> You will be like one sleeping on the high seas, lying on top of the rigging.
>
> "They hit me," you will say, "but I'm not hurt! They beat me, but I don't feel it! When will I wake up so I can find another drink?"
>
> Proverbs 23:31-35

Those glossy pages and touched up images in the magazine promise me pleasure. She is there inviting me to come and have a good time. She is always smiling. She always says yes. But there's not really a person there. It's an illusion. A beautiful bubble that will burst any second. After a momentary high, I'll soon be left with the feeling of emptiness, guilt, and shame. This is awful. I hate it. I detest being a part of it. I abhor what it does to me. I hate the grip that it has on me. And then, just like the drunkard in Proverbs 23:35 who longs for another drink, my craving induces me to go back and take another look.

Jeremiah 2:13 states:

> "My people have committed two sins: They have forsaken me, the spring of living water, and have dug their own cisterns, broken cisterns that cannot hold water."

The scriptures show us what our life experiences have already revealed—we are all thirsty. The problem is when we try to quench our thirst with the wrong things. Like the sparkling bubble floating in the air, these pleasures look like they will give us what we want and need, but we end up with an empty cistern and no water to quench our thirsty souls. We need to look to the living fountain where we will discover the clear spring waters which only the Lord can offer us.

The Bible is God's book, the book of truth. The Bible explains how temptations work in James 1:13-15:

> When tempted, no one should say, "God is tempting me." For God cannot be tempted by evil, nor does he tempt anyone; but each one is tempted when, by his own evil desire, he is dragged away and enticed. Then, after desire has conceived, it gives birth to sin; and sin, when it is full-grown, gives birth to death.

It is so easy to rationalize, minimize, and justify our actions. How many times have I done what Adam did when confronted with his sin? Adam not only tried to pin the blame on Eve, he even implied God was at fault. How convenient to say: "The devil made me do it." Or "I only did it because my wife let me down once again". Or to rationalize that all men have this weakness and even when I try to resist, it's just no use.

The Bible is like a mirror placing us face to face with reality. The plain and simple truth is: God is not to blame, and my wife is not to blame. I did it because I wanted to, because sin looked appealing at the time. Just like the Bible says: ". . . each one is tempted when, by his own evil desire, he is dragged away and entice. Then, after desire has conceived, it gives birth to sin; and sin, when it is full-grown, gives birth to death."

When I told my wife one day that I looked at those pictures of naked ladies out of boredom, she saw right through me. She said: "Why didn't you decide to look at pictures of horses or sunsets or race cars to relieve your boredom?"

Several years ago, I attended a class on sin and temptation where the speaker referred to desire as the "grandfather of death". Desires give birth to sin and sin gives birth to death. What insight! Why was I sick and tired of being sick and tired? I had given in to my desires and was reaping the consequences of my mistakes.

Willard wrote this in the Renovation of the Heart (p.122):

> "Feelings are, with a few exceptions, good servants.
> But they are disastrous masters."

I had placed my feelings and my desires on the throne of my heart. What cruel masters they are! I let my feelings rule my life and my life was a wreck as a result. Desires which are out of control will quickly lead to sin, and the wages of sin is death (Romans 6:23).

For thirty years I went through my days taking care of my responsibilities. I kept up with my work with the church. I raised our kids and helped around the house. I thought I was a good husband because I never had an affair. My excuse was, "all I did was look at pictures". I gave my wife flowers from time to time. On the outside, I looked like a Christian and a nice guy. But my wife says I didn't smile very much, and our marriage had become more of a business partnership than a loving friendship. I had become enslaved. My mind had been captured. I allowed my feelings and desires to drag me away and entice me. And I was suffering the consequences of my actions. I was being swallowed up by the quicksand of desire.

The apostle Paul described this devastating problem in 1 Timothy 6:9-10. Here Paul talks about the longing to be rich, but the same could be said of all of our carnal appetites:

> Those who want to get rich fall into temptation and a trap and into many foolish and harmful desires that plunge people into ruin and destruction. For the love of money is a root of all kinds of evil. Some people, eager for money, have wandered from the faith and pierced themselves with many sorrows.
> 1 Timothy 6:9-10

This is exactly what happened to me regarding lust and porn. These harmful cravings plunged me into ruin and destruction. The love of those pictures, of the captivating naked ladies, pierced my soul with many sorrows. I fell into the trap of foolish and harmful desires and harvested a myriad of noxious consequences.

In the book of Genesis, God talks to Cain, after Cain became upset with his brother Abel, but before Cain kills Abel:

> Why are you angry? Why is your face downcast? If you do what is right, will you not be accepted? But if you do not do what is right, sin is crouching at your door; it desires to have you, but you must master it.
> Genesis 4:6-7

I think that last part describes what we are up against. Sin is crouching at my door. It desires to have me. I must master it. A friend of mine often says there is always a fixed amount of time between the thought or desire and the action. We must wage the battle during this window of time. In the past, when I habitually gave in to my weakness, the amount of time between the thought and the fall would be minimal and I believed I could not stop it. I felt powerless.

Now, as soon as the desire or thought pops into my head I work to "master the thought". I move to eliminate it immediately. I know that otherwise, I will end up dominated by it. So I work to act quickly and decisively. Without a doubt this strategy is essential and is one of the major keys to breaking free from this sin that had entangled me for so many years. With the Lord's help I worked to take every thought captive one day, one hour at a time.

What makes a temptation tempting? I've mulled this over in my head over the past fifteen years. Why am I not tempted to smoke a cigarette or to drink a beer? I see those things and I don't give them a second thought. Some people struggle for years to give up these habits. The difference lies in the desire. I am only tempted by the things I desire. I believe we create, or at least we permit our own temptations.

If this is the case, then the key to victory in this battle against sin and temptation is to attack our desires. It is essential to work at changing or controlling our desires. Today I can't tell you I'm no longer tempted in the area of lust, but the degree to which I am tempted has diminished dramatically. God created us as beings with many capacities. Change is not easy, as you already know from your own experience. How many people sign up at a gym in January with a determination to get in shape, but by March have already lost their drive?

Yet, in the Bible God promises to always provide a way out when we are tempted to sin:

> No temptation has overtaken you except what is common to man. And God is faithful; he will not allow you to be tempted beyond what you can bear. But when you are tempted, He will also provide the way of escape so that you may be able to endure it.
> 1 Corinthians 10:13

Change is possible. This is not an impossible task. Sin comes along and offers what looks enticing. And like a fish looking at the worm in the water, we can't see the hook that lies underneath. Through prayer and by focusing on what we know to be true and right, over time we will see the worm but remember the hook and all of the pain it will bring. By intentionally focusing our thoughts on good things, our desire for what is wrong will diminish and no longer run rampant, dominating our minds. One of the greatest blessings I've gained now that I've found this new freedom is to have a clear head, with clean thoughts.

It is up to me to recognize my own weaknesses and know where the danger lies. The fact is, temptations begin inside of my own heart. It is essential for me to look honestly inside of my soul and admit that I am only tempted when the desire to sin dwells within me. This means it is essential for me to develop a strategy to replace those cravings for sinful activities, with a desire to seek the Lord. This transformation in my thought process will not happen in one day or in one week or even in one month. But modifying my thoughts is the only way to develop a new life, a life worth living.

John Owen said, "Be killing sin or it will be killing you." Temptations cannot be toyed with. The hook is always there to ensnare us and destroy us. But with God's help, over time, we can work to kill these desires that lead to sin. The Bible gives us this ray of hope in the book of James:

> Resist the devil, and he will flee from you.
> Come near to God and he will come near to you.
> James 4:7

If your thoughts are bad tenants, evict them before they destroy the house. Kicking them out and keeping them out is a full-time job, especially in the beginning. Yet as time goes on and you acquire new habits, you will find this whole process gets much easier.

Today you can learn from my mistakes. You can begin your journey to freedom today. Right now you can begin your new life by filling your heart and your mind with the Lord and everything He has to offer.

Matthew Henry wrote:

> "The joy of the Lord will arm us against the assaults of our spiritual enemies and put our mouths out of taste for those pleasures with which the tempter baits his hooks."

The best way to avoid the hook is to find your satisfaction and pleasure in Jesus. Then the hook of lust will have no power to lure you away from the Lord. Counterfeit joy is no match for the true joy which only the Lord can offer.

When you and I find our joy and satisfaction in the Lord, it will be easy to spot the deceptions sin throws our way. By faith, Moses refused to be known as the son of Pharaoh's daughter. He chose to be mistreated along with the people of God rather than to enjoy the fleeting pleasures of sin (Hebrews 11:24-25). The eyes of faith reveal the good and beautiful life the Lord offers, and they also expose the ugliness and fleeting nature of worldly pleasures.

Points to Ponder

Questions for Discussion Groups

1. What makes a temptation tempting? What are some temptations you find difficult to overcome? How have these temptations been a problem in your life?

2. Is it true that "Feelings are, with a few exceptions, good servants, but they are disastrous masters"?   Explain.

3. Read 1 Corinthians 10:13. How can the truths in this passage help you find victory over temptation?

4. What practical steps will you take to "be killing sin" in your heart?

Chapter Ten

Pre-Programmed Feet and Eyes

Remember how I told you that seeing pictures in the magazines at my cousins' house had caused a rush of excitement that led me to seek the same titillating feelings again. Those feelings led me to walk into a convenience store as a teenager and pick up a men's magazine off of the top shelf and thumb through its pages. The musty smell of that store and the fragrance of the glossy pages in the magazine have stuck with me to this day. Why did my feet keep carrying me back every chance I got? Why were my eyes always on the lookout for a location where these magazines were accessible, where I might take advantage of an opportunity to leaf through those pages one more time?

A few years after my wife and I got married, we moved to a large city. There, the magazines I wanted to peruse were sealed up inside of plastic bags. So what did my eyes do? They found a used bookstore where copies of old magazines were piled up on a table and anyone could pick one up and take a look. And coincidentally almost every time I needed to go downtown, my feet just happened to take me right in front of that bookstore and straight back to the table with those magazines. Of course, my problem really had nothing to do with my toes or my ankles. My desires were out of control. In spite of the fact that I proclaimed with my mouth that I was a man of God who was seeking to live a pure and clean life, I was actually programmed to seek out pornography. I had done this so many times that my feet, my eyes, and my hands seemingly did all of this on their own.

I learned from Jon Marsh's course that these routines can be termed "rituals" or ingrained routines that feel like a compulsion. Past experiences have convinced me that when I begin the ritual by going downtown, I will end up going into that used bookstore once again. It feels as if it is inevitable.

Here's an example of how one person broke down one of their sexual rituals:

Mike is a married father of two. He is just starting out in recovery. He describes his problem this way: *"I can't stop surfing the Internet for porn".*

Mike's Ritualistic Elements for a Specific Porn-Viewing Event:

1. Made several sexual advances towards the wife, she rejected me.
2. Felt sorry for myself; felt anger/frustration over marriage.
3. Experienced an urge to relieve myself through masturbation.
4. Began looking forward to my wife going to bed.
5. Wife went to bed; had to ensure that she was asleep.
6. Began the process of preparing the environment for secret porn viewing.
7. Began searching the Internet for porn.
8. Came across an image of two cheerleaders kissing.
9. Began fantasizing that I was with them.
10. Began masturbating.
11. Orgasmed.
12. Went into 'clean-up mode' — erasing history files and tracking information from my computer
13. Felt a sense of accomplishment at having had a successful experience without being caught.

There is a point of no return in any given ritual, where you know that you are going to complete it. While you may try very hard to pressure yourself through guilt and shame not to act out, deep inside, you know that eventually, you are going to carry out this routine or ritual. After all, it's what you always do.

The newest books in the Holy Bible are nearly 2,000 years old. And the book of Proverbs is something like 3,000 years old. That's why I'm so amazed by how relevant these writings can be. Proverbs chapter 7 presents this fascinating story:

> For at the window of my house, I looked out through my lattice.
> I saw among the simple ones.

I discerned among the youths a young man void of understanding, passing through the street near her corner, he went the way to her house, in the twilight, in the evening of the day, in the middle of the night and in the darkness.

Behold, there a woman met him with the attire of a prostitute, and with crafty intent. She is loud and defiant. Her feet don't stay in her house. Now she is in the streets, now in the squares, and lurking at every corner.

So she caught him, and kissed him. With an impudent face she said to him:

 "Sacrifices of peace offerings are with me. Today I have paid my vows. Therefore I came out to meet you, to diligently seek your face, and I have found you. I have spread my couch with carpets of tapestry, with striped cloths of the yarn of Egypt.

I have perfumed my bed with myrrh, aloes, and cinnamon.

Come, let's take our fill of loving until the morning.

Let's solace ourselves with loving. For my husband isn't at home.

He has gone on a long journey. He has taken a bag of money with him. He will come home at the full moon."

With persuasive words, she led him astray. With the flattering of her lips, she seduced him. He followed her immediately, as an ox goes to the slaughter, as a fool stepping into a noose.

Until an arrow strikes through his liver, as a bird hurries to the snare, and doesn't know that it will cost his life.

Now therefore, sons, listen to me. Pay attention to the words of my mouth. Don't let your heart turn to her ways.

Don't go astray in her paths, for she has thrown down many wounded. Yes, all her slain are a mighty army. Her house is the way to the grave, going down to the rooms of death.

Proverbs 7:6-27

This is a story about "a young man void of understanding", a guy who set his feet on autopilot. I think he probably would have told himself that he was just going out for a stroll, to get some fresh air. But the truth is that his feet took him straight towards the house of another man's wife. Later he might tell someone that he was the victim in this story. Yet nobody forces him to do what he does. He goes of his own free will.

Had he been to her house before? Maybe. But something about this story makes me think this is the first time he actually talks with her. Yet it appears to me that he had heard about her. I think he had probably fantasized about how an encounter like this might turn out. And I believe this was not the first time he had walked in that direction and allowed his eyes to search for this woman who had come to occupy his thoughts.

This young man imagines he is going to have a fantastic time. He assumes his dream is about to come true. After all, isn't this what every red-blooded man longs for? He doesn't realize that he is easy prey. He can't see that the person he is hoping to seduce already has everything planned out. She is the one who is going to trap and capture him.

She comes out to meet him. She's dressed to kill. Her feet never stay put. She is also pre-programmed for these fatal encounters. She is the Huntress, but she too is a victim of sexual addiction and sin. She lurks, she holds and she kisses. And as if all of this were not enough to reel in her fish, she uses her words to convince him that all is well. This will be an unforgettable evening. "My bed has the finest linens, the scent of the best perfumes, and my husband won't be back for ages." Her smooth talk captivates him. He is like a steer heading for the slaughterhouse.

Welch puts it this way in Addictions (p 56,57):

> "What started out as a somewhat hopeful walk
> ended in much more than he could have
> imagined. Yes, there was pleasure for a
> moment. The young man was purposeful in his
> pursuit of it. But it was the pleasure of an
> animal eating meat from a deadly trap. Little
> did he know that he had walked past sexual
> pleasure and had a one-way ticket to the

chambers of death. His sensual banquet was, in reality a banquet in the grave."

Look at those last three verses, written 3,000 years ago. What do they have to teach you and me in the 21st century?

> Don't let your heart turn to her ways.
>
> Don't go astray in her paths, for she has thrown down many wounded. Yes, all her slain are a mighty army.
>
> Her house is the way to the grave, going down to the rooms of death.
>
> Proverbs 7:25-27

Straying feet are a disaster waiting to happen. A heart that is easily turned aside by the seductive voice of desire and passion will turn us into victims and force those who think they are mighty to their knees. If there were a vast throng of people heading down this highway when the book of Proverbs was written, how many millions are on this same highway today? It's time for all of us to wake up and get RE-programmed feet, eyes, and brains. Today's the day to begin teaching our feet the dance of life, not death!

King David lived about the same time as the book of Proverbs was written. His son, King Solomon, wrote many of the proverbs contained in this book. The Bible tells us this story in the book of Second Samuel:

> In the spring, at the time when kings go off to war, David sent Joab out with the king's men and the whole Israelite army. They destroyed the Ammonites and besieged Rabbah. But David remained in Jerusalem.
>
> One evening David got up from his bed and walked around on the roof of the palace. From the roof he saw a woman bathing. The woman was very beautiful, and David sent someone to find out about her. The man said, "She is Bathsheba, the daughter of Eliam and the wife of Uriah the Hittite." Then David sent messengers to get her. She came to him, and he slept with her. (Now she was purifying herself from her monthly uncleanness.) Then she

2 Samuel 11:1-5

I'll confess that I might be reading something into this story
that's not there. But I think King David had pre-programmed feet.
Verse two tells us that one evening David got up from his bed and
walked around the roof of the palace. Then from the roof, he saw
a woman bathing. How many times had David done this before?
What did David expect to see when he looked down from the roof
of his palace onto the rooftops below?

I assume that if Bathsheba was taking a bath on her rooftop,
this was a common thing to do in those days. Wouldn't David know
he might just "happen" to see someone? David already had several
wives. Why in the world did David's feet take him up to the roof
and why did his eyes spot the naked lady? How long and hard did
David stare at this bathing beauty? And of course, that's just the
beginning of this story. David wasn't content to simply be a
voyeur. He sent someone to find out about her. How long did that
take? Wasn't there enough time for David to stop and think and
come to his senses? And even when he discovered she was a
married woman, married to a man David knew and respected, he
took that next step and sent messengers to fetch Bathsheba. How
could a man of God perpetrate such a monstrous act?

I wonder, in the years to come, how many times David replayed
this scenario back in his mind? If only I had stayed in my bed that
night. If only I had looked the other way. If only I had glanced at
her, but quickly gone back into my room. If only I had
remembered my other wives. If only I hadn't tried to find out more
about her. If only I had stopped when I found out she was
married. David had so many opportunities to slam on the brakes.
He could have stopped at any point. But I think David was already
hooked. He allowed his passions to become his master and he paid
an extremely high price for his sins for the rest of his life.

Having eyes that wander and feet that roam can lead to
disastrous consequences. Not only is lust a sin against God and
against a person made in His image, but it can even become a
crime. My appetite to look at and lust after female bodies could
have led me to voyeurism. How close did I come to crossing this

line? What might I have done if presented with the right (or wrong) opportunity? The desire to be desired and looked at could easily lead someone to become an exhibitionist. How embarrassing would this be if and when this person got caught in the act? Look where these sins might possibly lead!

And of course, it is not uncommon to see in the news where an adult, a man or a woman, became so wrapped up in his or her own selfish desires, that they initiated a sexual relationship with a person under the age of 18. Stop and consider for a minute all the dreadful consequences that giving free rein to lust can spawn. Scary stuff, isn't it? Just thinking about all of these possibilities makes me shudder. But just as the alcoholic needs to face up to where his problem might eventually lead him, the wise person will wake up and realize that to toy around with lust is like playing with fire. Which means getting burned is a very real possibility! Ouch!

Points to Ponder

Questions for Discussion Groups

1. What jumps out at you when you read Proverbs 7? Why?

2. Can you identify patterns in your behavior where you go into "autopilot mode" and do things you will later regret?

3. What concrete steps can you take to avoid sin in the window of time that lies between considering the temptation and actually committing the act?

Chapter Eleven

Lies I Told Myself

Lies are illusions, mere fiction. $2 + 2 = 4$ It is a fact. If I think that I have the ability to jump off a building and fly, that lie could lead to my death. The law of gravity is the truth, an undeniable fact.

How did I remain trapped on the hamster wheel of addiction to pornography for so many years? I heard lies and believed those lies. And the worst lies of all are the ones we tell ourselves.

As long as I considered those lies to be true, I was never going to break free from this sin. This is one place where I used my journal. As I wrote I worked on identifying these false beliefs or false "truisms".

Jesus said the truth will set us free. Among other things I believe this means that to live a life worth living we have understand what is real and what is false. Part of the work of recovery is uncovering the lies and replacing the lies with the truth.

So what are some of the lies, the illusions which kept me trapped in the compulsive cycle of lust and porn for well over 30 years? I'll list just a few of them here. Perhaps you can help me add to this list.

Lie #1: I'm going to quit. Just one more time and then I will give this up for good.
Truth: This went on for decades.

Lie #2: I know I will eventually give in so it might as well be now. I could fight the urge all day and waste the day or I could just act out now and move on with the rest of my day.
Truth: Urges pass. Feelings come and go. In order to develop new, healthy habits, I will need to overcome these destructive urges and move forward in purity, one hour at a time.

Lie # 3: Sex is my greatest need.
Truth: I could live a fulfilled life without sex. Many people have.

Lie #4: I have a higher sex drive than most people.
Truth: When I stop "feeding the beast" then my sex drive returns to "normal" levels. In fact, what is "normal" in the 21st century is not really normal because we are surrounded by provocative material in the media. In reality, a simple smile and a hug from my wife make me feel much better than looking at pictures of porn and masturbating. I'm tired of all these lies and pray that I will find my way to freedom.

Lie #5: Just a quick peek or a short impure thought is normal and natural. What I am doing isn't really "pornography". I'm just admiring the beauty of the female body – part of God's creation.
Truth: God wants me to avoid all forms of lust and maintain a clean mind 24 hours a day. God condemns adultery committed in the heart.

Lie #6: They're just pictures, not real people. Nobody is getting hurt. I'm not cheating. I'm not really lusting because I don't want to be with them. I just want to look at them.
Truth: I am turning a person into an object to be used for my pleasure. My wife feels like she's not good enough. She feels betrayed. I get so wrapped up in the addiction that I can't think of anything else. Everyone is getting hurt. Objectifying a woman is dehumanizing and degrading, both for her and for me. Am I no more than my lusts and desires?

Lie #7 (now this contradicts #6) I want to stop and I'm going to stop but I can't stop. This force that drives me to look is irresistible. I can't help myself. I know I will eventually give in, so it might as well be now.
Truth: I always have a choice. Every time I looked, I made a decision to give in to my passions and cravings.

Lie #8: Masturbation makes me feel good and relieves tension. It will stop my craving for porn.
Truth: Nobody explodes or dies from lack of orgasm. Masturbation feels good for a few seconds but afterward I feel worse than I did before. It's a dismal cycle of destruction. Giving in to cravings only

increase the cravings. It's like an alcoholic saying "This harmless glass of beer will stop me from craving whiskey".

Lie # 9: My wife doesn't give me what I need. She isn't available often enough and she puts everything else before my needs, blah, blah, blah. Therefore, I'm entitled to act out. What my wife doesn't know won't hurt her.
Truth: Knowing that I had been choosing my porn girlfriends over her was almost more than she could bear. I was being extremely selfish and self-centered, focusing almost entirely on my feelings.

Lie #10: Everyone does it.
Truth: Yes, millions are caught up in this perversion, but that doesn't make it normal or good. God doesn't grade sin on a curve. How many people are addicted to drugs or tobacco? Is that something you want for yourself or your children?

Lie # 11: I am strong enough now in my recovery that I can shift my boundaries and watch movies with nudity, mindlessly surf the net, spend hours clicking links on YouTube, etc.
Truth: All of us need to avoid even a hint of sexual immorality (Ephesians 5:3). We need to establish strict, crisp boundaries to protect ourselves from sin. Complacency is often the first step to relapse.

Lie #12: Discussing my emotions with others will make me seem weak, and will cause my friends to like me less.
Truth: It takes courage to admit our mistakes. Seeking help is an act of wisdom. People respect those who are willing to be vulnerable and change.

Lie # 13: Porn makes me happy. It will satisfy me.
Truth: It is never satisfying. I always wanted to look at the next picture. Just one more. Using porn induces a hunger for more, More, MORE! Afterward I feel degraded, guilty, ashamed, and emotionally walled off from the world. All alone. It's like being in a personal prison.

Lie # 14: I'll grow out of this porn habit. I'll quit after I get married or after my next birthday.
Truth: I remained in this endless cycle for almost 40 years.

Lie #15 I can beat the addiction by myself.
Truth: I never did. See #14.

Lie #16 If I say this prayer with enough conviction I will be free from this addiction forever.
Truth: Of course, there is power in prayer. God can do all things. But I have to want to change and take the steps necessary to seek change. Sanctification and spiritual growth require discipline and effort on my part.

Lie #17 I can live two lives. The porn life and the life I present to the world.
Truth: I am one person. Porn will bleed over into every corner of my life, rotting my soul and destroying everything that is good about life.

Points to Ponder
Questions for Discussion Groups

1. What lies have you been telling yourself? Why?

2. Have you identified the truth that dispels the lies you've been telling yourself? How will this make a difference in what you do day by day?

3. What are some other lies you would add to this list?

Chapter Twelve

Fake or Genuine?

A while back my wife and I traveled to a foreign country. We were at a big tourist attraction and as we left the site there were several small stores selling souvenirs and other items which they thought would appeal to visitors. One shop was selling replica watches and had up a sign which read: "Genuine Fake Watches For Sale". What can you say? At least they were honest!

Perhaps you have heard it said that men give love for sex and women give sex for love. And if by this someone means that in general men place more importance on the act of sexual intercourse than women do, I imagine it's true. Probably the average woman longs for romance and feels the need to be held and cherished. But I believe men need genuine love every bit as much as women do. I have not looked at the statistics, but I'm pretty certain that most crimes of passion are committed by men. We all need real love, genuine love, someone to value us, someone to grow old with, a person who cares.

Not too long after I confessed my involvement with pornography to my wife, she told me I had a choice to make. I could either say goodbye to all of my porn girlfriends and renew my commitment to her, or she would divorce me and let me enjoy my life with those other women. I told her that even if she decided not to give me a second chance, I was still going to continue my quest to live a life of purity, free from the grip of pornography. Everything pornography has to offer is counterfeit. It's an illusion. Sure, there is a thrill and a flash of excitement. Pornography offers enough titillation to send me and millions of others running back for more. But it has nothing to offer which really satisfies; nothing enduring, and definitely nothing to be proud of. Absolutely nothing that's really worth having.

When we think about choosing a marriage partner, picking a spouse based solely on a pretty face, great body, or any other physical attribute is foolish. A relationship founded exclusively on physical attraction is bound to get boring before long. (Not to mention that nobody will remain young forever.) How much better is it to be married to your friend, to a person you can count on, someone you respect?

I was talking with a friend who also found his way out of the grip of pornography. Today as he looks back at his participation in this habitual sin, he says he doesn't even know who that person was who did those things. He told me:

> "I'm sickened and revolted by who I became, and for what? What did I get out of it? Certainly nothing good, that's for sure. To me, it is shameful and embarrassing."

I found the following in a book called Lust Virus, which is now out of print:

> "Lusting is anti-man. It is not discipline and maturity. It keeps me a boy with adolescent desires. I remain immature.
> Lusting is anti-sexual. Not real sex, not healthy sex.
> Lusting is anti-woman. It turns a person into an object.
> Lusting is anti-love. Love is giving and sacrificial. Lusting takes and is selfish.
> Lusting is anti-human. It takes a human being and turns them into something to be used and abused. It transforms a person into a mere animal.
> Lust is all about me. Wanting more only leads to wanting more.
> Lustful eyes make me look at a woman and put a market price on her based on her body."

In his book "False Intimacy" (p.25), Harry Schaumburg explains:

> "Sexual addiction isn't just an issue of sex or even of external behavior: It's a byproduct of loneliness, pain, the self-centered demand to be loved and accepted regardless of the

consequences, and a loss of vital relationship
with God."

I'm sure you will agree, now is the time to stop lusting and start
loving. Today is the day to stop thinking about yourself and to start
thinking about others. It's time to quit making selfish demands.
Now is the time to be a friend who finds pleasure in giving rather
than taking.

God's plan is always best. God is love and he made us with a
need to be loved and so that we would love him and others. I
don't believe I have ever met a person who did not feel a longing to
be loved, valued, respected and appreciated by other people.

Schaumburg's book showed me how people believe pornography
is the easy way out; I can have a "relationship" without any
investment on my part. Those women in the pictures and films are
always ready and glad to see me. They don't care if I help around
the house or if I came home with a smile. I don't have to listen to
them tell me about their problems. These fictitious girlfriends are
ready and waiting to please their man. Yet this is all fake, one big
fat lie. I'm simply looking at dots on a screen, there is no person
there who loves me or cares about me.

Not to mention that I never stopped to realize the women in the
photos are real people with real needs. Someone is taking
advantage of them. Someone is using them to make a profit. The
porn industry can care less about this person being used and
abused. And to some degree as a viewer, I am taking part in this
exploitation. I need to remember that this lady is a human being.

This is all bogus love, just one more lie that springs from the
father of lies. The fact that there are dozens, if not hundreds, of
books, courses and support boards for people who want to
abandon pornography is proof that love is a thousand times better
than lust. Lust seems to fulfill a need for a few moments, but it can
never genuinely provide what it promises. It ends up hollow,
empty, and dry. Lust is an extremely lonely road to travel. Just
ask anyone who has gone down this road for a few miles.

Pornography is wrong because it is anti-relational. No love is
present when one person is using the other person. The root
problem of this sin (and many other sins) is pride and selfishness. I

want what I want because it makes me feel good right now. My selfishness pulled me away from my family. It made me blind to the needs of others. It prevented me from being the type of person I want to be, the man God intended for me to be.

After I discovered pornography on the Internet, I looked forward to moments when I would be home alone, without my wife or our children in the house. I was elated because I would have the opportunity to indulge my selfish desire for another fix. As I think about this now, it sounds so tragically sad and totally appalling. How could I prefer to be with some colored dots on a screen over being with my own family? Since confessing my sin to my wife, she revealed how she used to wonder if I wouldn't be happier living all alone, without anyone around to bother me. What had I become? Where was my selfishness taking me? What a dismal commentary on me!

In a commencement speech he delivered at Kenyon College in 2005, entitled "This is Water", David Foster Wallace stated:

> "In the day-to-day trenches of adult life, there is actually no such thing as atheism. There is no such thing as not worshipping. Everybody worships. The only choice we get is what to worship. And an outstanding reason for choosing some sort of God or spiritual-type thing to worship . . . is that pretty much anything else you worship will eat you alive. If you worship money and things, if they are where you tap real meaning in life, then you will never have enough. Never feel you have enough. It's the truth. Worship your own body and beauty and sexual allure and you will always feel ugly, and when time and age start showing, you will die a million deaths before they finally plant you."

Today I understand how pornography is self-worship. It is such a heartbreaking business, leading those involved to die a million deaths. Pornography is about me loving me. It's the unholy trinity of me, myself and I. It's me doing something for me because I want to do it because the excitement gives me a rush! As I write these words, they cause me to stare into the mirror and want to vomit. What a loathsome condition! Me kneeling down before the altar of self; me not caring about anyone else but me. There is no joy there. No peace. No fulfillment. No satisfaction. Just a great big giant hole that's getting bigger by the second. Looking in this mirror made me really, really scared. Participating in pornography is plunging headlong into the dark pit of no return.

I need and want genuine relationships and true intimacy. Of course, genuine love will require effort on my part. I will have to spend time with people, and sometimes they will not respond the way I want them to respond. But without a doubt, it's more than worth the effort. Who wants a fake diamond when they can own the bona fide article? Who wants to cuddle up to a glossy photo when they could have a human in their life who cares about them and enjoys being with them?

A friend of mine says we all have what she terms "soul holes". I've heard other people say we all have a God-shaped hole which only He can fill. In 1670, Blaise Pascal wrote:

> "What else does this craving, and this helplessness, proclaim but that there was once in man a true happiness, of which all that now remains is the empty print and trace? This he tries in vain to fill with everything around him, seeking in things that are not there the help he cannot find in those that are, though none can help since this infinite abyss can be filled only with an infinite and immutable object; in other words, by God himself."

Only God with his love is able to fill the infinite abyss in your soul and mine. People seek thrills of all kinds. Pornography is one of many illusions that people use in an effort to find joy and satisfaction. But of course only our Maker can offer us true happiness.

G. K. Chesterton said:

> "The man who knocks on the door of a brothel is seeking God."

What was it that keep going back to pornography for all of those years? Obviously, I was trying to find something. I was using lust and excitement in an attempt to fill the emptiness within my being. It certainly wasn't working. Instead of quenching my thirst, I just kept getting thirstier!

In Confessions, Augustine of Hippo said succinctly:

> "Thou hast made us for thyself, O Lord, and our
> heart is restless until it finds its rest in Thee."

Only when I learn to die to my desires for false love can I truly live. Only as my heart longs for Jesus, will true love triumph over the tempter's false promises. When I grow to value the Lord's incalculable worth, offers of temporary pleasure will be seen for what they really are. The joy I feel as I experience Jesus' love deep within me, will vaccinate me against the assaults of hollow thrills. To love pornography is to buy into the lie that lust is better than Jesus, fake is better than real, false is better than genuine and temporary is better than eternal.

I find what C.S. Lewis wrote in "The Weight of Glory" (p. 26), to be exceptionally insightful and helpful:

> "If we consider the unblushing promises of
> reward and the staggering nature of the
> rewards promised in the Gospels, it would seem
> that Our Lord finds our desires not too strong,
> but too weak. We are half-hearted creatures,
> fooling about with drink and sex and ambition
> when infinite joy is offered us, like an ignorant
> child who wants to go on making mud pies in a
> slum because he cannot imagine what is meant
> by the offer of a holiday at the sea. We are far
> too easily pleased."

What a travesty to settle for mud puddles when we could enjoy a vacation by the sea! But that is exactly what I had been doing. How many hours did I waste seeking joy and satisfaction from pornography? The longer I looked the emptier and lonelier I felt.

The human soul was created to relish and savor the fullness of Christ. Nothing else is big enough to fill the hole in our souls the way God intended. Only the Lord is ample enough to cause lust to loosen its grip on my soul. The cure for our pitiful addictions is to be overwhelmed by the preeminence of Jesus in all things.

After he retired from his counseling career, Carl Jung was asked how he helped people get well. His response is quite enlightening:

> "Most people came to me with an insurmountable problem. However, what happened was through our work together they discovered something more important than the problem and the problem lost its power and went away."

Who is this something more important? If you are like me, you know and love the 23rd Psalm, one of the best-known passages in scripture: "The Lord is my Shepherd; I shall not want." Or if we put it in the affirmative: "The Lord is my Shepherd; He gives me everything I need. He makes me lie down in green pastures. He leads me beside the quiet waters. He refreshes my soul. Even though I walk through the darkest valley, I will fear no evil, for you are with me; your rod and your staff, they comfort me."

Without Him I am empty. Without Him, it is all a farce. I don't want imitation love. I don't want a hole in my soul. Only He can make me whole. Complete. Satisfied. Jesus is the way, the truth, and the life! Jesus isn't just better; Jesus is the BEST!

Points to Ponder
Questions for Discussion Groups

1. Talk about the difference between lust and love.

2. How is selfishness at the root of every addiction? Explain.

3. What are some of the things you have used in an attempt to fill your "soul hole"?

4. How will you take concrete, practical steps to set your mind on the Lord and draw closer to him? How can you incorporate these practices into your daily routine?

Chapter Thirteen

Can God Use This For Good?

It's never right to do something wrong. And bad is never good. I certainly don't thank God for my long, painful and perverse involvement with pornography. I'm ashamed of what I did for so many years, and for not seeking help sooner. I wish I had never gotten involved in this sin and had never put my wife through so much torment. I plead with everyone who is caught up in this cycle of lust to get help immediately.

Nonetheless, today I can see how God can bring something good out of evil and my inexcusable mistakes. One of my favorite stories in the book of Genesis is the story of Joseph in Egypt. It is a masterful story of redemption.

While still a teenager, Joseph who is his father's favorite, is betrayed by his own brothers and sold as a slave. Yet in Egypt, with God's help, Joseph rises up to be Pharaoh's, right-hand man. In Genesis 50:20 Joseph tells his brothers: "You intended to harm me, but God intended it for good, to accomplish what is now being done, the saving of many lives." My interpretation is that God can use evil and transform it into something good. Or in other words, God can mine something valuable out of a pit full of muck.

Willard said:

> "What God gets out of my life is the person I become. What I get out of my life is the person I become."

I believe I am a better person now as a result of my struggle to fight my way out of this compulsive addiction than I would have been if I had never faced this challenge. The strain of this undertaking has, at times, been overwhelming, yet I believe it has been a time of growth. This process is helping me improve as a person. I hope I am becoming a man of character.

In James 1:2-4, we are told:

> Consider it pure joy, my brothers and
> sisters, whenever you face trials of many kinds,
> because you know that the testing of your faith
> produces perseverance. Let perseverance finish its
> work so that you may be mature and complete, not
> lacking anything.

It's difficult to find a person who really can welcome trials. Yet trials are the only way we can grow stronger. The person who wants to build up their muscles needs to work out and lift weights. As they sweat and strain their muscles grow larger and stronger. Of course, this is true with regard to our character. I should never have put my wife through all of this ache and agony, however, she too has grown as a result. She is now prepared to help other people who face similar trials.

I found there's nothing like ending up in the bottom of a pit to help me appreciate the One who is there to save me. I know full well that I can't do this alone. I remember reading the short but direct Breton Fisherman's Prayer: "Dear God, be good to me; the sea is so wide and my boat is so small." I sure can't lick this problem alone. I need help. My boat is tiny. I need the Lord. When my pain helps me look to the only One who can heal my pain, then perhaps my pain isn't totally bad.

Raising my hand and saying out loud that I chose to be selfish and to put my own feelings and emotions above almost everything else shows me how weak I am. Admitting my mistakes and the fact that I went back and fell into the same slime pit time after time reveals to me how utterly helpless I am. All of this should keep me humble.

I've always thought of myself as a hard worker and a good provider for my family. In my own mind, I was a faithful husband and a dedicated Christian. Nevertheless, as the prophet states in Isaiah 64:6: "all of my righteous acts are like filthy rags." I was more concerned about my own pleasure and feeling good for an instant than I was about anything else. How can I ever say that I am better than anyone? Before I judge others, I have to say with all clarity and honesty: "There but for the grace of God, go I."

I think most of us find it easy to look down on others. It's common to somehow think we are better than they are. But when we look in the mirror and see not only the errors we have committed, but stop to think about other acts we might have carried out, given the right circumstances, how can we ever feel that way? Having faced my own failures definitely gives me empathy for others who fail. My areas of weakness may not be the same as their areas of weakness, but I know what it feels like to fail. When I am honest with myself, I can't really find a good excuse for my actions. So, who am I to look down on a fellow struggler?

The greatest blessing for me was when I reached the bottom of the barrel is that I was forced to look is UP. Down at the bottom of the barrel I discovered without a shadow of a doubt that I do not have the answer. I need help and I need it very badly. My case is hopeless, and my case is urgent. I need a Savior!

It shouldn't be this way, but I sometimes find it easy to minimize my mistakes and think some of my sins are not really so bad. In reality, every disobedience is like telling God "No! I'm going to do it my way, I'll do what I want because I'm in charge here." Since this is true, to tell a little lie, talk about someone behind their back, or cheat on a test are all cases of rebelling against God. However, none of those things feel as wrong or as bad as pornography and lust. These actions on my part reveal my depraved nature. When I see how low I can get, it makes me appreciate God's grace and mercy infinitely more!

Staring at the evil in my own heart and understanding that Jesus died for sinners like me moved me to tears. One of my favorite passages in all of scripture is Romans 5:6-8:

> You see, at just the right time, when we were still powerless, Christ died for the ungodly. Very rarely will anyone die for a righteous person, though for a good person someone might possibly dare to die. But God demonstrates his own love for us in this: While we were still sinners, Christ died for us.

God's love for us transforms us. That is the nature of divine love. It is not that we are so lovable that God can't help but love us, rather God loves us by His own choice, not because of something we did. I know that I don't deserve His love, yet He offers it just the same. As the apostle, John wrote:

> This is love: not that we loved God, but that he loved us and sent his Son as an atoning sacrifice for our sins.
> 1 John 4:10

How do I feel today? Extremely grateful! Eternally thankful! He rescued me. He forgives me. He accepts me. He strengthens me. He is always with me.

I'm not proud of my mistakes. It seems I had to come to know and understand what it means to be lost before I could truly appreciate the tremendous gift of being found and pardoned. Having taken a peek at darkness causes me to appreciate the light that much more! Having looked evil in the eye, fills my heart with gratitude for His goodness, His love, His grace, His compassion, His mercy, and His faithfulness.

Since the Lord is ready and willing to forgive us, we need to accept and receive his grace and learn to forgive ourselves. Francis de Sales (1567 – 1622) wrote:

> "Have patience with all things, but chiefly have patience with yourself. Do not lose courage in considering your own imperfections but instantly set about remedying them – every day begin the task anew."

God's grace and mercy are available to you and me through His Son and our Savior, Jesus Christ. There is no reason for us to get down or give up. Our Lord offers us a new day. The apostle Paul in a letter to the church at Corinth composed a long list of ugly sins and then tells them in 1 Corinthians 6:11:

> "And that is what some of you were. But you were washed, you were sanctified, you were justified in the name of the Lord Jesus Christ and by the Spirit of our God."

No matter how much I botched up, in spite of my rebellion and disobedience, there is still hope for those who repent and seek the

Lord. You and I can be washed and justified, in spite of where we've been.

The name 'Satan' means accuser. Our enemy wants us to believe there is no use trying any more. He does his best to convince us to give up. He tells us we have gone too far and the Father will never take us back. But the word of God declares that the Father welcomed the prodigal son back home with open arms, and even threw a welcome home party (Luke 15:11-31).

Satan toils incessantly to sow his seeds of fear and doubt into our hearts and minds. Our enemy says, "Look at your sinfulness". God says, "Look to Jesus, the author and finisher of your faith" (Hebrews 12:2). Jesus, our Savior, came to defeat the devil and to set the captives free. (Hebrews 2:14-15)

I don't know what wrongs you may have committed. Perhaps you were involved in prostitution or had a series of affairs. You may have taken advantage of another person against their will. No matter how dreadful your mistakes, there is forgiveness. You can start anew. His grace reaches lower than your worst mistakes.

George Herbert wrote this poem about 400 years ago:

> LOVE bade me welcome; yet my soul drew back,
>   Guilty of dust and sin.
> But quick-eyed Love, observing me grow slack
>   From my first entrance in,
> Drew nearer to me, sweetly questioning
>   If I lacked anything.
> A guest,' I answered, 'worthy to be here:'
>   Love said, 'You shall be he.'
> 'I, the unkind, the ungrateful? Ah, my dear,
>   I cannot look on Thee.'
> Love took my hand and smiling did reply,
>   'Who made the eyes but I?'
> 'Truth, Lord; but I have marred them: let my shame
>   Go where it doth deserve.'

'And know you not,' says Love, 'Who bore the blame?'

    'My dear, then I will serve.'

'You must sit down,' says Love, 'and taste my meat.'

    So I did sit and eat.

In this poem, love represents Jesus. Look how Jesus sees you. You may feel that you are unworthy, "not enough," but the One who loves you looks at you through the lens of love. He sees you as who you can be, as the person he intended for you to be. And he is the one who invites you and me to sit down and eat with him, to be with him.

Jesus extends the same invitation in the final chapter of the Bible:

> "The Spirit and the bride say, "Come!"
>
> And let the one who hears say, "Come!"
>
> Let the one who is thirsty come; and let the one who wishes take the free gift of the water of life."
>
> Revelation 22:17

What is the key for you and me to finally escape the prison of habitual sins? We need to find our peace, happiness, and fulfillment in Jesus. When we are at home with our Lord, enjoying the living waters he offers us, we will no longer search for fulfillment anywhere else.

May Jesus be our everything, today, and tomorrow and forever!

Points to Ponder
Questions for Discussion Groups

1. Read James 1:2-4. How have you grown spiritually as a result of trials and tribulations you have faced in your life?

2. Talk about how your difficulties and problems have helped draw you closer to God.

3. How does remembering your own weaknesses and failures help you be more understanding and compassionate in relationship to others?

4. How does knowing you have been forgiven keep you growing and moving forward?

5. Pause now and think about Jesus offering living water. How does that make you feel? How does this fact inspire you want to share this blessing with other people you know?

Chapter Fourteen

Hope-Less or Hope-FULL?

Pornography was my Achilles heel. I had tried so many times to change and failed every time. When I told myself that this time was going to be different, another part of me replied in an instant, "Don't kid yourself. You will be right back at it again before you know it." Deep down in my soul, I felt I was doomed to repeat yesterday's mistakes today, and then do the same thing again tomorrow. No matter how sorry I was for the wrongs I had committed, or how convinced I was that I needed to do what was right, nothing ever seemed to change.

Maybe you have experienced the same sense of despair. I know some people are always worried and anxious. They worry about their job, or about their kids, or about their health or lack thereof. Worry has become a way of life. Jesus said not to worry about tomorrow, but there are so many unknowns. So much can go wrong. I'm afraid of what might happen. How can a person learn to find peace and to rest in God's hands? Some people are so worried about worrying that they have lost all hope of finding a new life.

Everyone chooses an online name on the support board where I kept my online journal. One man picked MrOuch, another Backstabber, another ScaredAmI, and another StillStruggling. One wife called herself EmptyAndDestroyed, another CompletelyDone, another selected IAmBetrayed, and another Hopeless. My wife chose the name "Devastated".   People caught up in pornography have often gotten to the point where the whole idea of hope seems remote, distant, unbelievable and unattainable. Things are really bad and there is often not much light at the end of the tunnel. I had definitely felt that way many times.

Every now and then my wife and I carry on a friendly banter where I tell her I am an optimist and that she is a pessimist. She always replies that she is not pessimistic, just realistic. I know firsthand that transformation does not come easily, and I have witnessed countless guys who have claimed that they were going to make an about-face, but their desire gradually fizzled out. Who am I to look down on them? How many years did I waste, trapped in this cycle of hopeless despair? The reality is that change is an enormous challenge and requires hard work, plenty of dedication and help from others. Nonetheless, change is possible! There is hope!

I can live without many things, but I cannot live without hope. If there is no light at the end of the tunnel, I'll just give up in despair, and then curl up in a ball and die. Hope is what keeps me going. Hope is what helps me believe in a better tomorrow, that it really is possible to live a life with no regrets. I'm so sorry for the hundreds of hours I wasted looking at women made in the image of God in order to lust after them. I regret more than words can express, the heartbreak and agony I have inflicted on my wife because of my selfish actions. But I believe that with God's help those days are behind me. Today the sun is shining and the skies are blue. Tomorrow's forecast looks good too! I am no longer without hope. I am full of hope.

Of course, my hope does not rest in my own strength or abilities or knowledge or determination. Thirty plus years of failures certainly disqualify me as the superhero who is going to swoop in and put everything right. My hope rests on the firm foundation of the One who created all things and on his Son who died to pay my debt and rose from the grave to soundly defeat the father of lies and to set the captives free.

I believe we often feel like we are "not enough". We think, "If people knew the real me, they could not possibly like me". I was certain of this when it came to pornography. That's why I never worked up the courage to tell anyone about my struggles. Well, Jesus knows me through and through. He knows all of my dirty secrets, yet Jesus loves me anyway. He loved me so much that he gave his life to rescue me. In spite of my weaknesses, failings and rebellious nature, Jesus thinks there is still hope for me. He believes in the new me. Jesus makes me hopeful!

Soon after Augustine's conversion, he was walking down the street in Milan, Italy. There he met a prostitute whom he had known most intimately. She called but he would not answer. He kept right on walking. "Augustine," she called again. "It is I!" Without missing a beat and with the assurance of Christ in his heart, he replied, "Yes, but it is no longer I."

Everyone who gives their life to Jesus Christ by repenting of their sins and being buried with Jesus in baptism has this hope.

> Therefore, if anyone is in Christ, the new creation
> has come:
> The old has gone, the new is here!
> 2 Corinthians 5:17

> I have been crucified with Christ and I no longer
> live, but Christ lives in me. The life I now live in the
> body, I live by faith in the Son of God, who loved
> me and gave himself for me.
> Galatians 2:20

This is exactly what I long for. To break free from the tug this addiction held on my heart. I yearn for freedom. I want to break the chains of slavery. I want to be able to hear temptation calling but to not even give it a second thought nor a second glance.

A dad whose son suffered from convulsive fits that sent him rolling on the ground and foaming at the mouth looked at Jesus and said:

> "If you can do anything, take pity on us and help
> us!" Jesus looked back at that dad and replied: 'If
> you can?' All things are possible to him who
> believes." Then the boy's dad exclaimed: "I do
> believe; help me overcome my unbelief!"
> Mark 9:23-24

That's where I am today. I'm ready to shout out loud and clear: "Lord, I believe! Help me overcome my unbelief!" How about you? Don't you want to shout out with me? Jesus is here. Jesus can help us. Jesus is the best!

When Jesus told his disciples "it is easier for a camel to go through the eye of a needle than for someone who is rich to enter the kingdom of God." His disciples were greatly astonished and asked, "Who then can be saved?" Jesus looked at them and said, "With man this is impossible, but with God all things are possible." (Matthew 19:26)

In his letter to followers of Christ in the first century the apostle Peter wrote in 2 Peter 1:3: "God's divine power has given us everything we need for life and for godliness." If God has given us everything we need, what do we lack? Nothing!

In reality, I always had everything I needed to beat this addiction. You have always had everything you need to turn your back on your habitual sin, find freedom and discover a new life. God is good and God is faithful.

The Spirit of God declares in Paul's letter to the church in Rome:

> If God is for us, who can be against us? He who did not spare his own Son, but gave him up for us all—how will he not also, along with him, graciously give us all things?
> Romans 8:31-32

God already gave us the most priceless gift of all. Jesus gave his life to rescue us from our sins. So won't He take care of us today and supply the resources we need to live a flourishing life right now? Of course, he will. In fact, if he hadn't already spoken to our hearts and given us a nudge in the right direction, we would still be blind to the darkness that had imprisoned us for far too long.

Can I live a life without lust? Only when I believe that all my needs are being met by the One who knows me the best and loves me the most. Drinking salt water will only cause me to be thirstier. Only the living water that comes from above can quench and satisfy my thirsty soul.

That's why Jesus is a million times better than porn or any other substitute. When Jesus spoke to a woman who went to draw water from a well, he told her:

> If you knew the gift of God and who it is that asks you for a drink, you would have asked him and he would have given you living water." Jesus answered, "Everyone who drinks this water will be thirsty again, but whoever drinks the water I give

> them will never thirst. Indeed, the water I give
> them will become in them a spring of water welling
> up to eternal life.
> John 4:10-13

The man who hopes to quench his thirst with porn and lust will forever be searching for one more thrill. The person who is searching for satisfaction through material possessions will constantly be running after one more purchase. But when Jesus fills my heart, he becomes in me a "spring of water welling up to eternal life." Only He is big enough to fill the hole in my soul!

This world has nothing to offer us. As the apostle Paul wrote to believers in Philippi:

> But whatever were gains to me I now consider
> loss for the sake of Christ. What is more, I consider
> everything a loss because of the surpassing worth of
> knowing Christ Jesus my Lord, for whose sake I have
> lost all things. I consider them garbage, that I may
> gain Christ and be found in him.
> Philippians 3:7-8

Jesus isn't just better than porn. Jesus is the best!

Do I have hope? Yes, I am hope FULL! My hope and my help come from the Lord the Maker of heaven and earth (Psalm 121). So what's my message to you? Your life can be different. You can live a life worth living. You can lay your head on your pillow at night and know that you lived a day with no regrets. With God, all things are possible (Matthew 19:26).

Today you can take another step towards the Light. You will need to ask for help along the way, but don't get discouraged. Every trial and obstacle you face will only make the prize at the end seem that much sweeter. Never forget that freedom is a glorious gift from above.

Points to Ponder
Questions for Discussion Groups

1. Is fear ever good? Explain.

2. What most gives you hope today? What Bible verses offer you hope?

3. What would you like your life to look like a year from now? Ten years from now? What steps are you taking today in order to walk into this reality?

Epilogue - Ghosts & Slaves

BREAKING FREE FROM THE HAUNTED HOUSE

> Above all else, guard your heart, for it is the
> wellspring of life. Proverbs 4:23

I regretfully admit that I did not do a very good job of "guarding my heart" for most of my life. One of the greatest benefits I have received since breaking free from my addiction to pornography is getting my thoughts back.

Let me compare my mind to a house. Formerly my house was a haunted house. The ghosts of addiction roamed the house freely and at will. I was never free from them. Those lovely images were always popping into my brain. They seemed to offer comfort, but they would never leave me alone and always cried out telling me that I needed to go back for more. I could never be satisfied. No matter how much I saw, I always wanted more. When I closed my eyes they would appear. When I lay my head on my pillow at night, the ghosts would never fail to haunt me.

Perhaps the saddest situation of all was when after looking at explicit material on a Saturday, I would be in church the next Sunday trying to sing praises to God or taking part in the Lord's Supper and have the ghosts of addiction roaming about in my brain. How could I betray my Lord like that? How would I ever break free? How many times had I promised that I would never go back there again, only to succumb to the deadly call of addiction one more time?

Today I live in a different house. This house is not dark and dreary. This house is bright and cheery. This house has many large windows and when I look out I see clear blue skies. Now I can close my eyes and pray, without having to worry about the ghosts from the past. Now I can lie down at night and reflect upon the events of the day or think about plans for tomorrow, without having to fight off the voices that cry out for more and more and more.

I love my freedom! That is why I can never allow myself to go back to that dark haunted house. I am very grateful for the freedom I have found, and I long to be free for the rest of my life. This is why I must resist every temptation that comes along and fight for my life with every ounce of strength that I possess.

In my beautiful and renovated house, there is always the danger of opening the front door or calling out the windows and inviting some ghosts which might be passing by to come in for a casual conversation, maybe just to catch up on old times. But I must never allow that to happen. What might seem innocent will quickly lead to a house that is infested with the ghosts and demons of addiction. Before you know it, the house can quickly lose its light and once again become horribly haunted, dark and dismal. Such is the enslaving nature of this and all addictions.

I have worked hard to free myself of these ghosts. In the early days of recovery, the images that had been burned into my brain kept reappearing all the time. I had given them free rule of the house. I had searched them out and invited them in. I considered these ghosts fun-loving friends who would comfort me and entertain me. Sadly, I learned over time that inviting them to come in was easy but asking them to leave was almost impossible. They had no desire to leave; as a matter of fact, they kept telling me that I should welcome their friends in as well. That's why a "zero tolerance" rule is the only way to fight them off.

The Bible provides plenty of advice for guarding our thoughts:

> Since, then, you have been raised with Christ, set your hearts on things above, where Christ is seated at the right hand of God. Set your minds on things above, not on earthly things.
> Colossians 3:1-2

> Do not conform any longer to the pattern of this world, but be transformed by the renewing of your mind.
> Romans 12:2

> Finally, brothers, whatever is true, whatever is noble, whatever is right, whatever is pure, whatever is lovely, whatever is admirable—if

I am what I think about, therefore I choose to think on things above. I choose to think on that which is true, noble, right, pure, lovely, and admirable. I choose not to allow the evil ghosts to gain a toehold in my brain. When one of these thoughts rears its ugly head, I chase it off immediately.

I'm tired of that haunted house. I much prefer the bright and peaceful house with windows that open up to a beautiful world. This is why I must follow the admonition in the Bible and guard my heart and mind, every minute of every day.

The ability to control my thoughts and to have my mind back is one of the greatest payoffs from recovery. When I was in the middle of my addiction I could not think straight. The ghosts of porn flooded my brain and it was hard to live in the here and now. Addiction is tormenting, unbearably stressful, tremendously time-consuming, and extremely draining.

When I consider the damage that addiction inflicts on my mind, my heart and my soul, I am motivated once again to stand strong in my resolve for purity. It's hard work to break loose, but every day it gets a little easier, even though the temptations still drop by and knock on the door when you least expect them. Drive the "ghosts and demons" away today and you will find that freedom lies just around the corner.

Remember, it all starts in our minds. Getting out of the rut is the hard part. Driving the first ghost out of the door may seem impossible. You must decide you are willing to pay the price and then get real with yourself and ask the Lord and brothers in Christ to help you. But when you do, you will find that the effort was definitely worth it.

A Willing Slave

As I look back on it all now, I was A WILLING SLAVE. Sin called and I answered. It was so charming, alluring and exciting. It felt so good. What could be wrong with that? Sin offered me pleasure and I wasn't hurting anyone. Sin made thousands of promises and I believed them all, but I don't think sin kept a single one. I really should have grown suspicious (but I didn't) when I was never satisfied, no matter how good it seemed at the time. I always wanted more. It was never enough.

While I did it all of my own free will, I certainly did not realize what I was getting into. I never dreamed that sin would hound me for years and years to come. But I can't say I didn't want to sin. How long could I go without thinking about sin? How many hours would go by before I would want to pull up those lusty thoughts and fondle them in my mind? I claimed I was enslaved by this entity sometimes called pornography or lust or desire. But when I face the truth head-on, I'm forced to admit that I sabotaged myself.

I kept telling myself that what I was doing was harmless. It was my private problem. I would take care of in due time. Yet I never told anyone. Not my wife. Not my best friend. Not a soul.

I took advantage of every opportunity I had to see just a little more and take another peek. I became an expert at looking over my shoulder, covering my tracks and not getting caught. Why go to so much trouble, if what I was doing was okay?

I was a slave for over 30 years. I don't know why I waited so long to finally tell someone. But eventually, I realized that I would never escape unless I got help. I was already in a very bad place and I perceived that this could easily get exponentially worse. That's when I knew I had to take action. Contrary to what I had told myself for all of those years, I was not a victim. I was a willing participant.

What looked so delightful and promising was actually very deadly and enslaving. It has the power to destroy me, my family and almost everything I value. Thousands and thousands of lives have been destroyed by this trap called lust. I don't want to be a slave, and with God's help, I will not be a slave any longer.

The Bible says in Romans 6:16-23:

> Don't you know that when you offer yourselves to someone as obedient slaves, you are slaves of the one you obey—whether you are slaves to sin, which leads to death, or to obedience, which leads to righteousness? But thanks be to God that, though you used to be slaves to sin, you have come to obey from your heart the pattern of teaching that has now claimed your allegiance. You have been set free from sin and have become slaves to righteousness.
>
> I am using an example from everyday life because of your human limitations. Just as you used to offer yourselves as slaves to impurity and to ever-increasing wickedness, so now offer yourselves as slaves to righteousness leading to holiness. When you were slaves to sin, you were free from the control of righteousness. What benefit did you reap at that time from the things you are now ashamed of? Those things result in death! But now that you have been set free from sin and have become slaves of God, the benefit you reap leads to holiness, and the result is eternal life. For the wages of sin is death, but the gift of God is eternal life in Christ Jesus our Lord.

How much better to be a slave to Jesus than to be enslaved by uncontrolled passions and desires. Living in sin only leads to regret and destruction. Doing what is right and good and true leaves me smiling, knowing that it was all worthwhile.

I don't have to be a slave anymore. Jesus came to give sight to the blind and set the captives free (Luke 4:18). I'm not doomed to give in to my selfish cravings, following every desire that pops into my head. God, in his great mercy, offers life to the dead and hope to the hopeless. His grace not only offers you and me forgiveness for all of our past mistakes; He also provides the means to do good works. This is our mission in life! Read Ephesians 2:3-10. We can become the kind of people who normally and naturally produce good fruit. Now that's a life worth living!

What About Masturbation?

Pornography and masturbation almost always go hand in hand. This was a huge problem for me. This is a controversial subject, even among Christians. As I see it, our primary sex organ is our brain. The excitement begins in my head as I think about my involvement with someone. She is beautiful and I am attracted to her body, thus I become stimulated. According to my understanding of sexuality, this is the only way to reach an orgasm. Therefore, I can't approve of masturbation, if Jesus said it is wrong to look at a woman with the intention to lust after her. Masturbation is impossible without the element of fantasizing and lust, and lust is a sin.

Along this line, C. S. Lewis wrote this in Collected Letters of C. S. Lewis (Vol 3, 758-59):

> "For me the real evil of masturbation would be that it takes an appetite which, in lawful use, leads the individual out of himself to complete (and correct) his own personality in that of another (and finally in children and even grandchildren) and turns it back: send the man back into the prison of himself, there to keep a harem of imaginary brides. And this harem, once admitted, works against his ever getting out and really uniting with a real woman. For the harem is always accessible, always subservient, calls for no sacrifices or adjustments, and can be endowed with erotic and psychological attractions which no real woman can rival. Among those shadowy brides he is always adored, always the perfect lover: no demand is made on his unselfishness, no mortification ever imposed on his vanity."

> Lewis concludes: "After all, almost the main work of life is to come out of ourselves, out of the little, dark prison we are all born in. Masturbation is to be avoided as all things are to be avoided which retard this process. The danger is that of coming to love the prison."

Appendix

If Jesus is the best, then what's the best way to get to know Jesus? We can't sit down and talk with Jesus in the living room, nor walk with him down by the Sea of Galilee. But when we read and meditate on what Matthew, Mark, Luke, and John wrote about the Son of God, he becomes real to us. We can get to know him there and learn from not only the words he spoke but from the way he acted and the way he treated others.

As you read through these books, one chapter at a time, ask yourself these questions. It will probably be helpful to write down your answers.

1. **Who is Jesus?** Not who is the Jesus you hear about on TV or learned about from a friend. But who is Jesus in the book of Matthew or in the gospel according to John?

2. **Why did Jesus come to earth?** What was his mission? What was his aim? What was most important to him? These statements may not be as obvious but if you look for them, you will find them.

3. **What does Jesus expect from me?** How does knowing Jesus change my life? I think the answer to this question is usually obvious once you have answered the first two questions. And of course, this is where the rubber meets the road. It doesn't do us much good to get to know Jesus and then continue doing what we always did. If the Son of God came to earth, what difference does that make in my life?

Spiritual transformation is the process of moving from the conformity to the world to conformity to Jesus. Spiritual growth means taking on the character of Christ. In order for this to happen, you and I need to fix our eyes on Jesus.

Our lives depend on what we choose to think about. It is essential to meditate on God's word. One of the best ways to do this is to memorize sections of scripture. Choose the ones that speak the most to you and give you direction in your life. You might want to begin with Psalm 1, 23, 40, 46, 103, or 121. Focus on the verses that you feel are most important. Other chapters might be Romans 8 or 12; 1 Corinthians 13; and Colossians 3.

You will need people in your life who can help you and as the 12th step of AA says, you will want to share your message with others. I believe that's one reason God established the church. We all need a spiritual family. Friends who can stand beside us. People to laugh with and shed tears with. I encourage you to choose your church carefully and wisely. Pray to God for guidance. Seek out a group of people who want to follow Jesus and the teachings Jesus passed on to the apostles, as recorded in the New Testament. Get involved. Find trustworthy brothers and sisters in Christ who can hold you accountable and help you as you strive to grow to become more and more like Jesus. This is the journey of a lifetime.

Obviously, there is always work to do as I seek to be the person Jesus wants me to be. We are all "in progress". I'm still dealing with a variety of sins (selfishness, pride, lust, anger, laziness—all mixed up in varying proportions). But the Lord is here beside me to help me. I have brothers and sisters in Christ, fellow-strugglers who can encourage me and point me in the right direction.

While I am not who I ought to be nor who I want to be or hope to be one day, I thank God I am not who I used to be.

You can reach me at onlywithhishelp@gmail.com

I'll try to reply.

If you found this book to be beneficial, please take the time to write a review. That will enable other people to find this book and get the help they need.

Thank you!

Hugh

Bibliography & Resources

THE PURITY PRINCIPLE by Randy Alcorn (Short and to the point.)

THE ENEMY WITHIN by Kris Lundgaard (Deals with fighting sin in general)

FALSE INTIMACY: Understanding the Struggle of Sexual Addiction by Harry Schaumburg (There is a wealth of knowledge to learn from this book.)

ADDICTIONS A BANQUET IN THE GRAVE by Edward Welch (Another scholarly work with a treasure of information from a biblical point of view.)

NOT JUST FRIENDS by Shirley Glass (Secular book for couples. A classic on the subject of betrayal)

For general Christian living:
RENOVATION OF THE HEART by Dallas Willard (One of my favorite authors)

INSIDE OUT by Larry Crabb (Very insightful and helpful)

Valuable Websites

https://2.bebroken.com/
https://www.affairrecovery.com/
http://www.battleplanministries.org/
http://followjesustofreedom.com/
http://www.porn-free.org/
https://www.provenmen.org/
https://puredesire.org/
https://www.purelifeministries.org/
http://recovering-couples.org/
http://www.recoverynation.com/
https://settingcaptivesfree.com/
https://stonegateresources.org/
https://www.xxxchurch.com/

If you enjoyed this book, please join Christian Indie Author Readers Group on Facebook.

You will find Christian books in multiple genres, opportunities to find other Christian authors and learn about new releases, sales, and free books.
https://www.facebook.com/groups/291215317668431/